D1243962

ADAM ELSHEIMER

1 *The Stoning of St. Stephen* (Cat. 15). Edinburgh, N

KEITH ANDREWS

ADAM ELSHEIMER

Paintings – Drawings – Prints

PHAIDON

Phaidon Press Limited, Littlegate House, St Ebbe's Street, Oxford

First published 1977
© 1977 by Phaidon Press Limited
All rights reserved
ISBN 0 7148 1770 8

Printed in Great Britain
Text printed by Aberdeen University Press Ltd
Monochrome illustrations printed by Alden & Mowbray Ltd, Oxford
Colour plates printed by Henry Stone & Son Ltd, Banbury, Oxfordshire

Robert Manning Strozier Library

FEB 10 1978

Tallahassee, Florida

To Jan and Ingrid van Gelder

CONTENTS

PREFACE

Whoever sets himself the task of tracing the sequence of historical events,
will find himself in a dilemma as soon as he is faced with a genius.   Max J Friedländer

The history of art contains certain figures around whom legends have grown, legends that have been difficult to see through so as to find the truth behind them. Lucas van Leiden, Giorgione, Watteau come to mind, and so does Adam Elsheimer. It will be noticed that all these artists died young, yet the impact of their work on succeeding generations was such that their names became attached to almost anything that had been produced even vaguely in their manner. In the case of Elsheimer the matter is further complicated by the fact that over the years people have formed in their minds a picture of what his work included and what it looked like. The chief element was a highly poetical rendering of nature, usually woodland scenery by the light of the moon or the sun or some artificial source of light, and this was thought to have come from the sixteenth-century 'Frankenthal School', a group of Netherlandish refugee painters who had settled in Frankenthal, not far from Frankfurt, Elsheimer's birthplace. Elsheimer was seen as one of their followers, imitating their style with tiny figures subservient, yet contributing, to an overall poetic, even mysterious effect. Such poetry was also thought to have been evoked at times—mostly in a series of gouache drawings—by a representation of pure landscape, incorporating only a few, if any, figures. It was this feeling for nature and the ability to interpret its moods which was taken to have been Elsheimer's special contribution to the idealized landscape-composition which later became the legacy of Claude Lorrain and Rembrandt and their followers, and which earned Elsheimer the name of 'the painter-poet'.

This image of the artist—only marginally true and hence misleading—seems to have emerged soon after Elsheimer's death and led to erroneous attributions as early as 1628 (Inventory of the Elector Maximilian of Bavaria). Even Hollar, to judge by the many etchings dating from the 1640s which bear the inscription 'Elsheimer invenit', seems on occasion to have been misinformed. The difficulty is increased by the fact that contemporary documents about Elsheimer are scarce and only a few early drawings bear authentic signatures and dates. Thus the whole oeuvre and its chronology has to be reconstructed from a highly subjective point of view, of which the two main criteria must be quality and stylistic consistency. Elsheimer's career tends to generate more questions than can be answered and, apart from the few cases where his authorship has never been questioned, there is fertile soil for speculation and legend. Each age created a new Elsheimer for itself, and it is time for a closer

look at the work in order to discover whether the accretions can be removed an
essential artist revealed.

As with all innovating geniuses, followers and imitators came quickly on the sce
even in Elsheimer's lifetime his own work often had to compete with that of min
who tried to imitate his unique language. Some works which have for many y
centuries, borne Elsheimer's name, I have felt unable to accept as autograph. M
have been briefly listed in the section headed 'Rejected Works'. Some of these I hav
discussed more fully in three articles (*Burlington Magazine*, September 1972 and N
and *Münchner Jahrbuch der bildenden Kunst*, XXIV, 1973). On the positive side it s
noted that, particularly since the memorable Elsheimer exhibition at Frankfurt in
a number of works have come to light whilst others have been rehabilitated after d
neglect, so that his oeuvre has been diminished and increased in roughly equal
Fuller details are contained in the relevant catalogue entries. It may never be possible
at universal agreement about all the works which have been attributed to Elshein
even among those presented here, some still bear an implied question mark. It i
important to define the oeuvre, to enable us to establish the special characteristics of Elsl
art and the qualities which made him the unique artist that he was.

I have assembled a sequence of works which I hope will not only be accepted as au
but will also be seen to form a convincing development within the fourteen years whi
the whole of Elsheimer's short career. I have not attempted to deal in detail with
artists whom he influenced, as this would fill another book. Collectors of Elsheimer's
appeared early on the scene and nowhere more persistently and passionately than
country, headed by Thomas Howard, Earl of Arundel. It is astonishing to note how m
the extant works were at one time in British collections, or are still there.[1]

The Elsheimer literature really began with Bode's revaluation in the 1880s and reac
climax with Weizsäcker's monumental three-volume monograph (the last volume
posthumously by Hans Möhle), the result of a lifelong study of the artist's life and
If today it is felt that Weizsäcker's connoisseurship was often faulty and that much
work has now been superseded, his research among archives and old catalogues is sti
basis of all Elsheimer scholarship. Hans Möhle undertook the catalogue of the drawir
task which Weizsäcker did not live to accomplish. If there has not been universal agree
with Möhle's selection and conclusions, it nevertheless remains the basis on which to
any new edifice. Willi Drost wrote a memorable monograph on Elsheimer in 1933,
years before Weizsäcker's first volume appeared, and his perception is truly admirable,
though he accepted works which need to be removed from Elsheimer's oeuvre. On the c
hand his book on the drawings of 1957 has deservedly attracted severe criticism for his er
connoisseurship and theories. Ernst Holzinger, one of Weizsäcker's successors at
Städelsches Kunstinstitut in Elsheimer's native city, did more than anyone to illumi
some of the subject-matter of paintings which up till then had been wrongly interpre
But it was the two memorable essays in *Simiolus* by J. G. van Gelder and Ingrid Jost, surv
ing the Frankfurt exhibition, that sent out a shock-wave through Elsheimer studies and

one to look afresh at all the works, and at all the suppositions and attributions that in many cases had been accepted as sacrosanct. In preparing the present book I have followed their example. Nobody working on Elsheimer can afford to ignore any of the publications mentioned above and I feel particularly conscious of a great debt to them.

Her Majesty The Queen has given gracious permission for the reproduction of Plates 3, 21, 22 and 109. All private owners and curators of public collections have, without exception, gone out of their way to give me all facilities to study the works under their care, and I should like to express my gratitude to them all. Numerous colleagues and friends have encouraged me in my work, and rather than list them here in a long and rather impersonal manner, I have acknowledged their contributions at the relevant point in the text and catalogue entries. However, I must name a few to whom I feel especially beholden. Malcolm Waddingham is a tiller of the same soil, with whom I have had many discussions and whose lively intelligence and keen eye make me feel doubly uneasy when I have come to different conclusions from his. Reinhold Hohl's thesis on the drawings of the period provided many valuable insights. In Rome, C. L. Frommel and Herwarth and Steffi Röttgen gave a great deal of their time to my problems, whilst Armando Petrucci and his wife helped to decipher some intractable documents I had found. C. P. Brand and Ian Campbell have corrected the translation of some of the Italian and Latin sources. My colleagues Kirstine Brander Dunthorne, John Dick and James Holloway were subjected to an almost daily barrage of Elsheimer problems and always responded with sympathy and enthusiasm. In addition, John Dick and John Brealey taught me all I know about the technical aspects of Elsheimer's painting methods. Colin Thompson discussed with me many problems and he also read and criticized the first draft of the text to the benefit of both its content and style. Jan and Ingrid van Gelder have constantly sent information and have endlessly helped and encouraged me with their friendship, and I have expressed my gratitude to them in the dedication. I should like to acknowledge the expert way in which Beatrice Morton has typed the manuscript, and furthermore I owe much gratitude to I. Grafe, Keith Roberts and Simon Haviland of the Phaidon Press for the great care with which they have seen the book through the press.

Finally I should like to acknowledge gratefully grants for travel and research provided by the British Academy, the Leverhulme Research Trust and the German Academic Exchange Service.

K. A.

December 1976

ADAM ELSHEIMER

The bare biographical facts, as they are known today, of Adam Elsheimer's short life are soon told. He was baptized in Frankfurt on 18 March 1578, the eldest son of a tailor (Doc. 1). He is said, probably correctly, to have been a pupil of the local painter Philipp Uffenbach (1566–1636), who himself had studied under the son of a pupil of Grünewald. Elsheimer is likely to have visited Strasbourg before 1596, in the company of Johann Vetter, to see Friedrich Brentel and the glass-painting studio of Lingg (see drawing, Cat. 28). In the second half of 1598 Elsheimer travelled, probably via Munich, to Venice (drawing, Cat. 30). In Venice he was associated with the Munich painter Hans Rottenhammer, who was then working there. By April 1600 he was in Rome (Doc. 2), where he settled for the remaining ten years of his life. In 1606 he became a member of the Accademia di S. Luca (see Self-Portrait, Cat. 26A) and after being converted to the Roman Church, he married in December of the same year a certain 'Carla Antonia Stuarda da Francoforte' (Docs. 3 and 4); she was possibly a member of a Scottish emigré family which had settled in Frankfurt, and had been married previously to Nicolas de Breul, a painter from Verdun, who had died only two months before. A son was born in 1608 (Doc. 7). (That there were several children, as Sandrart reported, is one of this writer's many fancies.) In the same household lodged an 'Henrico pictore' (Docs. 5 and 9), who has been identified as Hendrick Goudt (1573–1648), a Dutch artist who seems to have played a dual role of pupil and patron. According to Sandrart, Goudt had Elsheimer thrown into the debtor's prison for not delivering enough work. However, no documentary evidence for this story has been found. Elsheimer is said to have died soon after his release, apparently reconciled with and nursed by Goudt (Sandrart), and was buried on 11 December 1610 in the church of S. Lorenzo in Lucina (Doc. 10). An inventory of the possessions in the household, which his widow drew up eight days after his death, confirms the poverty in which Elsheimer must have lived (Docs. 11 and 12). In the signatures on the early drawings, he spelled his name 'Ehlsheimer', probably a phonetic rendering.

BEGINNINGS IN GERMANY

The visual arts in Germany, after the death of Dürer, Cranach and their followers, receded to a low ebb and did not revive for a century. The uncertainties of the time and the approaching storm-clouds of the Thirty Years War inhibited a vigorous and continuous patronage on a large scale. There were, to be sure, isolated centres of enlightened and occasionally feverish

artistic activities, such as the court of Rudolf II at Prague and the one in Bavaria, but F
for example, was not in the sixteenth century—and has never really been—in the f
as were centres like Nuremberg, from which a continuous stream of significant art e
For a short period around 1526, with the presence of Grünewald in the neigl
Aschaffenburg and with commissions in Frankfurt itself, the town gained a certai
reputation, whilst later on some of the Frankenthal painters actually settled in Frankl
a flourishing publishing trade which required engraved illustrations attracted artists
Amman. Uffenbach owned a collection of Grünewald drawings, which no dou
made available for study to his pupils, among them Elsheimer. And Uffenbach hir
some of his works (*St. Anthony; The Calvary*; Plates 102–3), followed closely the trad
the great era of German art of the early part of the century. He made copies aft
Dürer and Grünewald and one of his most important commissions, the altar-piece
Ascension (1599) in the Dominican church, was placed near Dürer's *Heller Altar* and v
it in shape and consciously based on it.

Although by 1599 Elsheimer had already left for Italy, it is clear that his apprent
was fundamentally within the German tradition, and any influence he may have re
from the Netherlandish Frankenthal painters was only marginal. This is amply demon
by the early works known to us. The idea of an overwhelming impact of the Frank
school (Plate 101) on Elsheimer, which past writers have consistently stressed, seems
fallacious, and it has done much to cloud the true picture of his development. In an
when reconstructing his oeuvre from the beginnings in Uffenbach's studio to the last
in Rome, it must be remembered that the span in which he was allowed to create w
more than fourteen years, so that the conventional framework of a gradual but clear dev
ment from early to late works becomes less meaningful than in the case of most other a

That Elsheimer studied with Uffenbach is a traditional notion, but it is not docume
However, it is very plausible, as Uffenbach was the principal native artist in Frankfurt a
time. He headed a studio and Elsheimer took part in ventures such as the Fran
Messrelationen, news-sheets reporting on world events which were published twice a
(in the spring and autumn) for the Frankfurt Fairs and for which Uffenbach and his assoc
supplied most of the illustrations (Plates 7, 10–11). The works which can be attribute
Elsheimer with some certainty at this stage are few and not of great significance. If what
survived seems rather slight compared with what was to come later, it shows neverthe
the German tradition in which he was brought up. The design for a stained-glass wind
(Plate 1) and the drawings for an *album amicorum* (Plates 2 and 24) show clear dependence
South German and Swiss prototypes, such as the engravings by Jost Amman and To
Stimmer, and make a journey to Strasbourg—probably in the company of the youn
Johannes Vetter, a glass designer—a distinct possibility. The older Vetter, was the head
the guild of stained-glass artists, and may possibly have been Elsheimer's first teacher. B
the young artists left drawings in an album which belonged to the Strasbourg pain
Friedrich Brentel, with whose style Elsheimer's early drawings have much in commo
Dürer's prints were either copied in oil (Plate 3), or adapted in original etchings (Plates 5–

The latter show the young artist battling with a medium that proved rather intractable to him and that he never really mastered, as even later etchings clearly show. However, Dürer was not looked upon merely as providing impulses for exercises, he also led the emerging artist to discover his own individuality: the *Heller Altar* (Plate 106)—at that time still in its original place in the Dominican church at Frankfurt—gave Elsheimer the stimulus for his first major surviving work. The little house-altar with *Scenes from the Life of the Virgin* (Plates 12–18) has in turn been attributed to Elsheimer, rejected and re-attributed, always with a certain unease. The shape of the six panels echoes that of Dürer's altarpiece, and the central section of the Ascension and Coronation of the Virgin is modelled very closely on the respective passage in the Heller Altar. However, there is a tenderness in the conception of the scenes and a filigrane delicacy in the handling of the paint which, in spite of areas of damage, reveal an artist of great individuality and sensitivity, even if as yet not of great experience. Elsheimer had here found his own language, and though it was developed and refined, it remained the same language, the same expressive organ of a receptive artist.

The originality is particularly noticeable in the treatment of the figures: heavily draped, mainly statuesque, yet with a refinement of expression right down to the smallest of them— these are characteristics that we shall continue to find in Elsheimer's works. These positive qualities far outweigh the more obvious weaknesses, which are most apparent in the middle panel (Plate 13), where the composition does not hang together but is split into various units and accents. These weaknesses appear more severe than they really are because a major loss of paint exaggerates the highlights against the still strong blue-green of the Virgin's cloak and against the surrounding angels. The lower figures, culled—even down to some of the gestures —from the same part of the Heller Altar, are too loosely organized to make a satisfactory composition. However, with fewer figures and a less complicated design, the scenes of the subdivided wings and especially the predella with *The Death of the Virgin* (Plate 14) have a tenderness and simplicity that could only have come from the hand of a painter of outstanding sensitivity.

The confrontation of the two women in *The Visitation* (Plate 16), the gentle wonderment of the two parents in *The Nativity* (Plate 17), and above all the group of sorrowing Apostles surrounding the dying Virgin are unique in their delicacy and intimacy. Dürer may have been the 'spiritus rector', but his inspiration has been absorbed and a new voice is here making itself heard. We also get in these panels the first glimpse of Elsheimer's use of landscape, not just as a foil for the figures but as an integral component in the rendering of the atmosphere of a scene: for example the tiny view through the door in *The Nativity*, and the wider prospect in *The Visitation*. The gently undulating hills and the spherical tree-forms are harbingers of things to come—passages which were going to be looked upon as hallmarks and were to be copied and adapted endlessly even during Elsheimer's lifetime. Although an imperfect work, it nevertheless provided a proving ground for a young artist who was still looking over his shoulder at his masters.

The little altarpiece also reveals another Elsheimer characteristic: the very simple, direct and literal way in which a story is told. Even highly dramatic and emotive incidents are

rendered with an unemphatic calm, which on occasion borders almost on gentle do[...]
There is usually a persistent and unhurried refusal to make any comment; no rhet[...]
elegiac meditation. An exception is *The Conversion of Saul* (Plate 20). Although st[...]
related to the altarpiece, it is a kind of 'Sturm und Drang' picture with a viole[...]
theatrical composition, unique in what we know of Elsheimer's oeuvre. The ce[...]
design seems to reflect the impact of a bomb, with horses and even the light scatte[...]
directions. Again, light is not used merely dramatically to enhance the general effect[...]
with great subtlety, to model some of the figures. This is achieved by silhouetting
against the light, so that body and drapery are shaped by the brightness. It is a met[...]
is much more effective on a small scale and that was favoured by those artist[...]
'miniaturists', whose technique Elsheimer used to some extent. This was already ev[...]
the Moorish King in *The Adoration* of the house-altar and it occurs again in the soldie[...]
right in *The Conversion of Saul*. The painting was obviously left incomplete, a circu[...]
which provides an opportunity to observe Elsheimer's technique, for the grey underp[...]
the ground with which he usually prepared his copper plates (unless they were 'sil[...]
shines through in several passages. This grey ground acted as a middle tone on wh[...]
colours were brightened or darkened as required.

The Conversion of Saul, stylistically and in the handling of paint, fits in well with the
altar and should be placed in the years of apprenticeship in Germany. The tumultuous
derive from prints by Baldung Grien, Lautensack, and especially Jost Amman, whi[...]
prostrate figure of Saul—almost like an exercise in foreshortening—is reminiscent of a s[...]
figure in Elsheimer's own stained-glass design of 1596 (Plate 1). How the vision in th[...]
which prostrated Saul, would have looked, had it been completed, can only be sur[...]
and this also applies to the similar passage in the other surviving painting of Elshe[...]
German period: *Jacob's Dream* (Plate 19). The massive, peasant-like figure of Jacob, recl[...]
in heavy, uneasy sleep on 'the stone he put for his pillow', is a direct descendant c[...]
sleeping soldiers in Dürer's and Uffenbach's *Resurrection* (Plate 105).

Again, as in *The Conversion of Saul*, proper judgement is impeded by the impaired c[...]
tion of the copper plate and the unfinished state of the painting. But enough can be se[...]
establish that it is an original work by Elsheimer and that it belongs to the early yea[...]
Germany. Much the best preserved and finished section is the woodland foliage on the[...]
Its rich darkness and almost jungle-like exuberance is one of the few signs of a pos[...]
influence of the Frankenthal painters; but this influence is only marginal and was in no s[...]
of paramount importance in shaping Elsheimer's style.

This group of paintings, drawings and prints is the sum total of what is knowr[...]
Elsheimer's early output. A convincing chronology is impossible to establish, but it seem[...]
least plausible that the three paintings can be considered as 'apprentice pieces' by an artist v[...]
had just emerged from Uffenbach's studio, who was imbued with the tradition of the ear[...]
German masters, but was already fledging his wings. Frankfurt was not a place where[...]
aspiring young artist of outstanding talent and extreme sensitivity could hope to develop a[...]
obtain adequate commissions. As with so many northern artists before him, Elsheime[...]

sights were directed south, towards Italy. After completing the rather exotic illustrations to the Spring edition of the *Messrelationen* in 1598, he left his native town, and must have spent a while in or around Munich, as another album-drawing bears witness (Plate 24). This depicts, appropriately enough, an allegorical representation of a young artist being presented to Mercury, the protector of the arts, with a picture within the picture dealing in emblematic fashion with the depressing prospects of lofty aspirations being dragged down by poverty. It proved to be a prophetic statement as far as Elsheimer's future life was concerned. Yet Mercury did lend him his support: Munich was on the road to Venice, the very centre which, ever since Dürer's days, has been the initial goal of northern travellers to Italy.

However, the strong and lasting echoes from artists such as Altdorfer and other Bavarian painters in Elsheimer's later works make it unlikely that he would merely have passed briefly through the Munich region on his way south. He must have lingered there for some time. Hence it may well be that he arrived in Venice not in 1598, as has hitherto been assumed, but later, and that he stayed only a few months rather than two years in the lagoon city.

VENICE

Flemings like Pauwel Franks (Paolo Fiammingo), Maerten de Vos, Jan Bruegel had all passed through Venice or had actually settled there. Lodewijk Toeput (Pozzoserrato) had established himself in the nearby Treviso, where the Munich-born painter Hans Rottenhammer had also worked for a time,[2] whilst other Munich artists had settled in Venice, notably Christoph Schwarz. Although documentation is sparse, it seems that foreign artists had a difficult time to establish themselves vis-à-vis the Venetian guilds and therefore, to a large extent, they found themselves dependent on the patronage of the merchant groups of their own nationality in Venice.[3] The best of these foreign artists took as much from their Venetian milieu as they contributed to it. Towards the turn of the century it was artists like Veronese, Tintoretto, the Bassano family and Palma Giovane who continued the great Venetian tradition of Bellini and Titian, and their large altarpieces in the churches and the vast cycle by Tintoretto in the Scuola di S. Rocco, with their glowing colours and sweeping dramatic compositions, were like text-book patterns for many of the younger painters who had crossed the Alps from the north. However, Venetian painting was not limited to large-scale works, for ever since Giorgione's smaller pictures, intended not for churches or palaces but for the homes of private collectors, a more intimate style had gone side by side with those public commissions. There was also a flourishing school of printmakers, again largely inspired by northern art, who worked in a small format, though often the large compositions of the great painters were made the subjects of these engravings. In much the same way, most of the northern painters attempted to reduce the monumentality which they found in the works of the great Venetians and to combine this with a northerner's concern for landscape. Their attitude to landscape derived from the tradition prevalent in the Netherlands, to which the Germans in particular added the more romantic mode of Altdorfer and other artists of the so-called Danube School. Venice was a fertile ground for such combinations, for landscape had been prominent in Giorgione's work, in the drawings and engravings of

Titian and Domenico Campagnola, and in the decorative backgrounds of \
frescoes in the Villa Maser.

In Rome too, the paintings of Girolamo Muziano, who came from Brescia, but
Venice—and the engravings made after them—as well as the landscape-prints by Hie
Cock of Antwerp, are further evidence of a widespread interest in landscape, hither
marginal activity of Italian artists. The two dominant figures in this field, howev
Jan Bruegel the Elder, in Italy between 1593 and 1597, and Paul Bril, resident in Ro
about 1580 till his death in 1626. Bril began his Italian career by painting landscap
in the Vatican, but his fame rests on a large series of small panels on wood and c
was also quite common for fellow artists to make use of such landscape specialists tc
the background for their own figure compositions (Hendrick van Balen with Jan
for example), and Rottenhammer too, after his first brief visit to Venice in 1589,
and Jan Bruegel in Rome and made use of both artists for the landscape background
of his paintings.

Rottenhammer must have returned to Venice about 1595, and he remained there
when he returned to Bavaria. It was to Rottenhammer that Elsheimer went when h
in Venice, probably sometime in 1599. Their exact relationship is not absolutely c
unlikely that Rottenhammer had anything approaching a full studio establishment
know of no real pupils of his in Venice and, apart from the altarpiece of *The Annun*
S. Bartolomeo (replacing Dürer's *Feast of the Rosegarlands*), most of Rottenhammer'
(*cf.* Plate 108) was on a small scale, unsuitable for pupil intervention. Furthermore, El
who had already the wonderful panels of the house-altar to his credit, is more likely
been a colleague than a pupil. How close their styles have on occasion felt to be is sh
the recent publication of *The Adoration of the Magi* at Hampton Court (Plate 109) a
of Elsheimer's, though it has borne a convincing attribution to Rottenhammer eve
was first recorded in the Royal collection at the end of the seventeenth century.[4] Tl
was, however, a close association is evident from those works which can confid
placed into Elsheimer's Venetian period: *The Flood* (Plate 27), *The Holy Family* (P
and *The Baptism* (Plate 28). Traces of Rottenhammer's influence can be found am
figures and especially the facial types in these paintings: the slit eyes, the prominent r
emphasis of the vertebrae in some of the nudes seen from the back. *The Flood* also I
Bassanesque characteristics (*cf.* Plate 110) and the other two paintings show the in
Veronese in the sweep of their composition and the richness of the draperies. These in
never appear to have overwhelmed Elsheimer, for they are fully integrated into work
seem like natural extensions of his own style, and the traces of Venetian paintings lc
they were seen through Rottenhammer's eyes.

What strikes one as new and remarkable is the role of landscape in these works: I
in *The Flood*, more prominent in the other two, with a combination of Danube-
exuberance and calmer southern modes. These are the first significant Elsheimer lanc
Not primarily a landscape artist himself, it is possible that Rottenhammer recommer
the young artist the theoretical considerations of landscape, as laid down by Lomazzc

11 *The Exaltation of the Cross* (Cat. 16). Frankfurt, Städelsches Kunstinstitut

sixth book of his *Treatise* of 1585 and given more practical application by Cristoforo Sorte's *Osservazione nella pittura*, which was published in Venice in 1580 and reprinted in 1594. In spite of much scientific and philosophical speculation, Sorte's book was intended—and was indeed used—as a manual for practical guidance.[5] He gives instructions for the rendering of the four seasons, storms, burning towns and night pieces. Two sources of light, for example from the moon and the torch (fol. 11), was a recipe which Elsheimer must have taken to heart (cf. *The Flight into Egypt*, Plate 91).

The publication of many landscape-prints, both Italian and northern, and their wide dissemination, was responsible for an intermingling of styles throughout Europe and for the familiarity of one country with the manner of another. Furthermore, the fact that most of the print-makers were also painters made it easy and natural for them to use the little copper plate interchangeably for engraving or as the support of a painting. Hence the scale of most of these paintings was small and the brush was of the finest, allowing the tiniest detail to make its effect on an extremely smooth surface. Muziano, Paolo Fiammingo, Jan Bruegel, Bril and Rottenhammer all used copper as a support for their paintings and Elsheimer himself had already painted on copper before he came to Italy. It is not clear for whom these small works were executed, who commissioned them and for what purpose they were intended. One can, however, be sure that some of them at least were destined as decorations for furniture, in particular for inlaying into cabinets.

Elsheimer arrived in Venice well qualified by his apprenticeship in Germany to adapt himself easily to the kind of work Rottenhammer was engaged on during his Venetian years: small pictures on copper depicting religious or mythological scenes, often with the background painted in by a fellow artist. Two religious paintings, today in the Museo Civico at Treviso, are documented—by dated inscriptions—as the combined works of Rottenhammer and Bril.[6] Although the attribution of the stylistically related Hampton Court *Adoration of the Magi* (Plate 109) has given rise to uncertainty, there can be no doubt about the *St. Christopher* of which the best extant version is in Leningrad (Plate 23). This is clearly an Elsheimer invention and must be a transitional work. It is difficult to decide whether the composition was conceived and executed while Elsheimer was still in Germany or whether it is one of the first fruits of his Italian sojourn. The massive figure of the Saint reveals the impact of Dürer (his woodcut, which was also the source of Uffenbach's etching of the same theme), and of the more sculptural figures to be found in Tintoretto paintings. The *St. Christopher* and *Jacob* are the most weighty and majestic single figures in Elsheimer's early work. Was it perhaps such figures which led Sandrart to report that Elsheimer began his career by painting big ('gross malen')—big, that is, within the small scale which had always been his chosen format?

The gnarled features of the Saint recur in the drowning man in the lower right corner of the painting which has always, and probably rightly, been considered as Elsheimer's first major Italian work: *The Flood* (Plate 27). In this one can see the first definite influence of Venetian art on Elsheimer, for the composition seems to be based on passages from a painting by Bassano (Plate 110). The figures are still 'Mannerist'—in particular the larger ones in the

foreground—and echo Rottenhammer to such an extent that, as in the Hamp
Adoration, one might be forgiven for wondering for a moment whether there h
act of collaboration. The youths climbing up the trees, and the people processing at
gait, which belies the dramatic and distressing situation described, will be foun
later Elsheimer works. The throng of figures is as yet awkwardly handled, anc
leaden sky, rent by flashes of lightning, gives any hint of an atmosphere of doc
groups and single figures, as well as in the animals in the background, one
Elsheimer's hand most readily by their delicate modelling, their individual chara
in spite of their miniature size, and the play of light on them. It is in fact the first ʃ
know by Elsheimer where light has a dominant role. It not only helps to create atɪ
but it plays among figures and trees, sky and water, and models each form. Liɟ
rationally conceived. Whatever is touched by it becomes luminescent as if it werɛ
source of light. It is the first 'night piece', a genre with which Elsheimer's name ·
associated through the ages. The prototypes are Altdorfer's nocturnal subjects and
tenebrist compositions. There was thus no need for Elsheimer to await the inf
Caravaggio in Rome, as has been claimed throughout the literature on Elsheime
case, with Caravaggio the source of light is never revealed, as it is almost invaria
Elsheimer picture. A dramatically lit scene, such as *The Flood*, was part of the
tradition which Elsheimer enriched with new impressions gathered in Venice.

Whereas in *The Flood* the landscape is merely a backdrop to the diagonal procɛ
The Baptism (Plate 28 and Col. Plate III) and *The Holy Family* (Plate 29) it plays a more
role, not only enveloping the figures, but fusing light and figures into an emotion
In these two paintings light is a divine, all-pervading force. It softens the pinpoint s
of the tree-lined hills against the sky, echoing the intimate, lyrical happenings in t
ground. The colourfulness of the whole conveys an impression quite new in Elsʃ
work. The grandeur of Veronese, here condensed into a tiny format, is overwhe
evident in the two main figures of *The Baptism*. Grandly conceived (in Sandrart's senɜ
are as yet static, as if too consciously posed. Their features and those of the seat
removing his shoe are all partly in shadow, and therefore less fully characterized tha
in the middle distance on the right. Here for the first time are the turbaned rider
soldier with the plumed hat, and the negro silhouetted against the light, that appear s
in later works. Oriental types were known to Elsheimer through figures in Dürer's
and from the prints of Jost Amman, such as the magnificent *Arrival of Ambassadors of th*
in Frankfurt (Plate 111). The bronzed bodies of the ring of putti and the angel hold
garment show clear Rottenhammer physiognomies: the protruding upper lip, th
slightly bent upwards, the widely separated eyes with the gracefully curved eyebrov
in particular the characteristically prominent modelling of spine and shoulder blade
most markedly in the dark-haired putto. But this group of angels is not exclusively Vɛ
or merely a derivation from Rottenhammer, it also shows clearly how much Elsheim
absorbed from Altdorfer during the time he must have lingered in and around Muni
Altdorfer's *Nativity*, Munich). However, what is totally original, one might say ;

sensational, is the treatment of the all-pervading light. Although Altdorfer and the later Venetians had used light as a dramatic, almost magic ingredient in their paintings, it was more often than not used like a spotlight on a stage, with a resulting theatrical effect. Elsheimer uses light as the *earlier* Venetians had done, as an agent which fuses nature and figures into one, defining forms as well as space. Less spiritual and less formalized than in Bellini and Giorgione, light with Elsheimer provides atmosphere and sets the scene for the figures. The sources of light are always clear: supernatural, natural (sun or moon), or artificial (torch), and there are often more than one within the same picture. Some hints of this were already perceptible in the small panels of the *Life of the Virgin*, but it begins to be triumphantly evident in those paintings which date from the time he spent in Venice.

The Holy Family and *The Baptism*, both with rounded tops, must have followed each other within a short span of time. The former still shows echoes of Altdorfer (the figure of Joseph in particular) and the types look more like those of Rottenhammer than of Veronese, as they do in *The Baptism*; hence that it is likely that *The Holy Family* was the earlier of the two. The landscapes are no longer mere backdrops, but envelop the figures and underline the mood of the scene. The colour is richer and more harmoniously handled than for example in *The Flood*. The ring of putti—a typical Altdorfer motif—has been choreographed into a daring serpentine swirl around the central ray of light. The richly brocaded robe of the Angel and the rendering of the elaborate, almost jungle-like trees and foliage are far more assured than anything seen in previous paintings. One might say that *The Holy Family* is Elsheimer's first truly mature work. The human situation, always of primary importance to him, is more sensitively rendered here, whilst one can sense his delight in the pure narrative, so vividly apparent in all subjects he treats. This was a gift that he exploited to the full—a northern and specifically German trait. Veronese's rhetoric, which had to make an effect from a distance, has been transmuted to a scale which would register from a closer range. To the task of compressing the monumentality of large frescoes and altarpieces, Elsheimer brought sensibility and patience, as well as the skill to work on the scale—and almost in the manner— of the old illuminators of manuscripts. He absorbed in a very short time what Rottenhammer and Venice had to teach him.

What made him leave Venice and settle in Rome is a matter for conjecture, like so much else in Elsheimer's life. Was it has own yearning for wider horizons and possibly more lucrative commissions? Was it Rottenhammer's suggestion, based on his own experiences in the Holy City only a few years earlier? Was it Paul Bril in Rome, whose collaboration with Rottenhammer on one and the same painting (Plate 109) that was sent to and fro bridged the distance between the two cities and whose feeling for landscape must have found a response in Elsheimer? All we know is that Elsheimer had reached Rome by April 1600 and never left it till his death ten years later.

ROME

Unlike most major towns of Italy, Rome never fostered a native school of art. It was always dependent, for longer or shorter periods, on the presence of artists from other regions of Italy

and from abroad. It has always been a whirlpool of artistic activities, of new i
experiments, and it acted as the magnet for lucrative commissions from the Pa
from the Church and from cardinals and princes. The hope of such patronage br
like Annibale Carracci, the young Caravaggio and Rubens to Rome around the
century. However, there were also members of the professional class who collected
local contemporary artists and who would also have been interested in the smal
pictures in which Elsheimer specialized. Among them was Johannes Faber, a do
Bamberg, who treated Rubens during a serious illness. He was the official herba
Pope and wrote a work on antique sculpture, as well as one on the animals of
America, in which, à propos the lizard, he makes a charming reference to E
Mocking of Ceres (see Cat. 23). It was to Faber's circle that Elsheimer found his wa
and his younger brother Philip belonged to it, and so did the volatile Kaspar
(Scioppius), a German Lutheran who was converted to Roman Catholicism and
vociferous propagandist for the Papacy both in Germany and Italy. Even in an age
polemics, he distinguished himself by the virulence of his writings against the Pr
Izaac Walton in his *Life of Sir Henry Wootton* called him 'a man of restless spirit and
pen'. Rubens, in a letter to Faber, seems to imply that it was Scioppius who was re
for Elsheimer embracing the Catholic faith. But Scioppius was also a man of
humanist interests and it is an attractive suggestion that it was contact with this c
led Elsheimer to some of the more recondite classical themes he was to tackle d
Roman years. The other person who stood close to Elsheimer was Paul Bril. He a
were two of the witnesses at Elsheimer's wedding and both owned paintings l
Although Bril began his Roman career by painting frescoes in the Vatican and Lat
fame, like Elsheimer's, rests on small-scale pictures on copper and wood. Whe
chronology has been worked out, it may well be found that the change of style so
in his landscapes after the turn of the century was in fact due to the impact of Elsl
presence in Rome. Such an influence was also hinted at by Dr. Faber. [8]

There is little documentary evidence about the collecting habits in Rome at this pa
period, but there must have been a demand for small cabinet-pictures, for the invent
the larger collections, the Barberini, Aldobrandini and Doria-Pamphilij, contain a
of them by artists such as Bril, Jan Bruegel and Elsheimer; whether these pictures are
correctly attributed remains uncertain, as the descriptions are often so vague as to be
in tracing particular works. Cardinal del Monte—Caravaggio's first patron—and C
Scipio Borghese owned paintings by northern artists and the latter appears to have
particular patron of them. [9] Otherwise no information has come to light as to the k
people for whom Elsheimer might have worked: no contracts of payments have been
and it may well be that none existed. It should not be forgotten that when Elsheimer a
in Rome at the age of twenty-two, he was hardly known and even later he was known
to a small circle and did not receive the kind of commissions like altarpieces and f
decorations, for which contracts and bills would normally have been drawn up. Hov
there were numerous collectors in Rome of these novel small, highly wrought ca

pictures, so that Elsheimer was able to obtain high prices for his works, as Sandrart reports. Yet his method of working and his temperament prevented him from completing enough to make a living.

Rome widened Elsheimer's horizon, his assurance increased and his choice of subject matter expanded. Among the earliest works which are likely to have originated in Rome, though they still depend in many ways on a northern, Bruegel tradition, are the two 'night pieces': *The Burning of Troy* (Plate 31) and *Paul on Malta* (Plate 30). Both works are in some sense extensions of *The Flood*, exploiting the drama of night skies, raging or sparkling fires and people caught up in natural disasters. Yet the tragic events are muted by genre details which on the face of it seem totally extraneous to the spirit and decorum requisite to such themes. The principal episodes are related with the precision of the born story-teller, but the calamities are embellished with incidental observations of such stark realism (like the ship-wrecked women in *Paul on Malta*, drying their clothes) that any Romans who saw these works must have been startled. Apart from the increased assurance in rendering such dramatic events, these two paintings display a greater skill in the handling and modelling of the figures than anything that had gone before. Hence one must either assume that some intervening works have been lost, or interpret such developments as a reflection of new stimuli which Elsheimer had received in Rome from the works of art—old as well as contemporary—which it contained or from the city itself.

Those paintings made by Elsheimer in Italy which have been considered hitherto contain either vague classical edifices or ruins. In the *Preparation for the Martyrdom of St. Lawrence* (Plate 33), he freely renders one particular building, the Temple of Vespasian. The figures have gained in stature and solidity, as if, for once, the northern miniaturist wanted to vie with the grander scale of his Italian fellow artists. The scene depicted is an uncommon one, for it is not the actual martyrdom of the Saint on the gridiron, which is usually portrayed, but the preparation for it. The gestures of the attendant figures imply that the Saint, contrary to tradition, refused to worship pagan gods. Hence the statue of a youthful Apollonian Hercules, to which one of the oppressors points. This may possibly have been a recollection of Titian's rendering of the martyrdom of the same Saint (Venice, Gesuiti), where an antique statue of Vesta figures prominently. The figures enacting the scene are grouped into the left foreground of the painting. Standing upright, yet without rigidity, they are sculpturally conceived and clothed in voluminous draperies, which add to a sense of monumentality. It may at first appear as if they were frozen in their movements but, as in a Gluck opera, the emotions have been stripped away and the simple action remains. The closely observed details of the costumes, as well as the luxurious plants of the foreground, and the richly orchestrated verdant background, were to inspire in particular Elsheimer's Dutch associates in Rome, such as Lastman, the elder Teniers and the Pynas brothers, and were eventually transmitted to Rembrandt. In this picture also, the two youths preparing the gridiron in the middle distance are the first of the subsidiary figures filling a space, yet essential to the narrative, which recur in various guises in many of Elsheimer's later compositions. Behind these youths in the *St. Lawrence* composition is a cavalcade of horsemen (reminiscent of Jost

Amman's *Riders with Attendants* from the third book of Paul Jovin's *Warhafftige*
. . . of 1570) and footmen with turbans and berets. These have been taken over,
variations into *The Stoning of St. Stephen* (Plate 46 and Col. Plate I), a stylistically re
and hence probably close in time.

Here the crowds of *The Flood* and *The Burning of Troy* have been marshalled
tightly-knit groups, without losing the feeling of a thronging mass of people. Th
the obvious delight in handling the narrative transmute the gruesome scene, by its
and colourfulness, into the miraculous incident it was. Elsheimer isolates the cer
by a theatrical spotlight of heavenly rays, which also catches some of the riders w
into the middle distance. Rubens was so fascinated by some of the figures—s
passive spectators—that he copied them in a drawing (Plate 118), regrouping th
new composition which was famous enough to have been engraved with th
'Elsheimer Inv.', and which had puzzled scholars until Dr. Ingrid van Gelder-Jost po
the connection with the recently rediscovered painting. The crowded compositio
downward sweep of the angel with widespread wings still contain echoes of
impressions, but the prominent, very sculptural figure of the semi-nude stone-thro
the typically Roman ruins in the background are evidence of Elsheimer's presen
Eternal City. It seems that the painting was owned by Paul Bril; but it is curious
entry in his daughter's inventory states that the landscape-background was by Bril h
The ruined arches and to some extent even the trees are reminiscent of Bril's styl
seems unreasonable to expect a second hand to have intervened in the tiny area cov
the landscape, and it must be assumed that filial piety had in this instance been taker
by Bril's descendants. Elsheimer, who produced the very similar, but much more ex
background in the *St. Lawrence* painting, would not have been in need to call on a colla
for the small section in the *St. Stephen*; however, it shows how very close were the s
the two artists. While it is likely that Elsheimer learnt from Bril, Dr. Faber's rema
suggests that Bril, during the last twenty years of his life, adapted his style to the ini
way in which Elsheimer incorporated landscape elements into his compositions.

The relationship with Bril was not the only possible influence which Elsheimer migh
undergone in Italy, and in Rome in particular. The names of Annibale Carrac
Caravaggio in particular have been cited in the literature: Annibale because of his imag
use of landscape, a novel extension to the largely figurative art to which Rome w
customed—less flamboyant and less fantastic than Bril's often bizarre composition
Caravaggio because of his predilection for strong contrasts of light and dark. It wou
foolish to doubt that a young artist, barely twenty years old, absorbed the works of
luminaries around him, in the same way as he had learnt earlier on from Dürer and Altd
or from Rottenhammer and the Venetians. But, as in the case of the Frankenthal paint
would appear that much too much has been made of the impact on him of the wor
Italian fellow artists which he encountered in Rome. The 'night pieces', the drar
exploitation of light or the absence of it, and the modelling of figures with light ca
observed in Elsheimer's works before he ever set foot in Rome or saw any of Caravag

paintings. Traces of this predilection for using light not merely as a decorative adjunct but as a positive agent in creating a composition can even be discerned in pictures he must have painted before he left Germany, and this trend was then fully developed in his Venetian works. The sources of Elsheimer's chiaroscuro stem from Altdorfer and Bassano and not from Caravaggio.

As to the 'poetic landscapes', mysteriously reflecting the moods of the people who inhabit them, these too had already figured to some extent in the little panels that make up the Berlin house-altar. Again they were developed through contact with the works of Altdorfer, the Venetians and that tradition from which also Paul Bril stemmed. Curiously enough, Annibale Carracci's own landscape style had its roots in the very Venetian prototypes which also helped to develop Elsheimer's inimitable rendering of nature. The elevation of landscape to something more significant than a mere foil to the narrative was a parallel phenomenon in both Annibale's and Elsheimer's Roman works, and whether one was aware of the other can only be surmised. Annibale favoured an idyllic, idealized landscape, Elsheimer a typically northern, wide expanse, often seen from a high viewpoint and often with wild 'romantic' vegetation. Carracci and his followers created landscapes in which figures were inserted as staffage, almost like an afterthought, which could be removed without the composition disintegrating, whereas Elsheimer's figures were conceived as an integral part of the landscape and are inseparable from it. This fusion of serene lyricism of narrative and landscape was Elsheimer's very personal contribution to European art and must have been fully formed by the middle of the decade, for it was being imitated by followers like David Teniers the Elder and the Pynas brothers, who returned to their northern homelands in 1605 and 1608 respectively.

It has been suggested that the modelling of the figures in Elsheimer's Roman works (for example the stone-thrower in the *St. Stephen*) was such an advance on what went before that it can only be explained by direct contact with the work of other artists. Saraceni in particular has been mentioned in the literature as having influenced Elsheimer, whilst at the same time he is supposed to have modelled the landscapes, which are such a prominent feature in many of his works (for example the Ovidian series at Naples), on Elsheimer's example.[11] Apart from the question whether Saraceni was in fact responsible for the very Elsheimer-like landscapes which feature in some of his paintings, it would seem strange that Elsheimer, once he was in Rome, should have needed to rely for the development of his figures on a Venetian-born artist who himself had only arrived in Rome two years before him. These seem futile arguments, for the type of the stone-thrower, for example, is certainly prefigured in Elsheimer's own work, for instance in the figure of Aeneas's son Iulus, carrying the torch in *The Burning of Troy*.

Elsheimer's Roman works can be divided into two categories: the multifigured compositions and those which concentrate on a few figures only or on a single one. Even if the exact dates and chronological order of these works cannot be established with certainty, it seems clear that *The Burning of Troy* was developed from the prototype of *The Flood*, whilst *St. Lawrence* led to *The Stoning of St. Stephen* and ultimately to the seven-part house-altar with *The Story of the True Cross* (Plates 47–54), probably the most ambitious work he

ever attempted, and further to *Il Contento* (Plate 71), his most elaborately orga
position. In a similar way, the early intimate scenes from the *Life of the Virgin* (P
foreshadow the series of *Saints and Biblical Figures* (Plates 55–63) which were painte
A fairly continuous line from early endeavour to maturity can thus be discerned.
famous remark that Elsheimer was a 'Römischer Maler deutscher Nation' cannc
sustained; he remained essentially a German artist who found himself working in

If, in the absence of any other surviving work, it might be said that Elsheimer
period had reached its climax in the altar with the *Scenes from the Life of the Virgin*, s
Italian period reached a turning point in his second, somewhat larger house-altar.
incidents of the discovery of the True Cross and its final elevation. This is a
consisting of seven separate copper panels and we know from a document how
were assembled, what each depicted and what the frame looked like (Doc. 14d,
There is no other work by Elsheimer of which such a full account of contemporar
has survived in the documents. By 1612 the little altarpiece was in the possession of
collector in Rome and was subsequently acquired, after some initial hesitation, by t
Duke Cosimo II of Tuscany, on the strong recommendation of his Agent, th
Agostino Tassi. Since two of the panels were, until not long ago, in the collecti
Dukes of Norfolk, it is likely that they reached England through Thomas Howarc
Arundel (grandfather of the 5th Duke of Norfolk), who was known to have e
works of art with the Grand Duke of Tuscany. All but two sections of the altarpi
now been recovered, so that a partial reconstruction of the whole is possible.

Stylistically the polyptych can be dated to the early years of the century, the til
Rubens was engaged on painting an altarpiece in S. Croce in Gerusalemme on ve
the same theme. It was his first major commission and had come to him from A
Albrecht of Austria in Antwerp—probably through Philip Rubens, the painter's
brother. Both belonged to the circle of Justus Lipsius, the humanist, classical philolc
re-converted Catholic, who had published a treatise on the significance of the C
Christian symbolism, ending, as Elsheimer did in the central panel of his altarpiece
'Laudatiuncula Crucis'—the exaltation of the cross. Thus the subject was 'in the air'
may be of significance in the case of both Rubens and Elsheimer, for pictorial represe
of the legend, and the Adoration of the Cross in particular, were fairly rare.

Elsheimer concentrated on the actual discovery of the Cross and its final return to Jer
as narrated in two separate chapters of Voragine's *Golden Legend*: beginning w
embarkation of St. Helena, continuing with the discovery of the Cross and ending w
entry of Heraclius into the Holy City—six panels grouped around the largest, central s
showing the glorification of the Cross by figures from the Old and New Testa
Compared with the *St. Stephen*, there are fewer attendant figures in each scene, the ac
more concentrated, and the landscapes are even more elaborately worked out. As
Berlin altarpiece, the events are depicted with a minimum of protagonists and with
decorum, objectivity and restraint. Once again, each scene shows Elsheimer's suprem
in compressing into the most confined compass the essence of an event, yet never

Detail from *The Empress Helena Embarking to Find the True Cross* (Plate 49)

Detail from *The Digging for the Cross* (Plate 53)

III *The Baptism of Christ* (Cat. 8). London, National Gallery

expense of vivid details, such as the carpeted plank over which Helena steps into the ship that will take her on her momentous journey; the woman enjoining silence on the uncomprehending children; the brawny workmen digging for the Cross; and the contrast between the sudden backward movement of the startled Emperor on horseback and the plodding attendants, unaware of the supernatural apparition of the Bishop and the Angels in the sky. This last detail shows that Elsheimer must have used another source in addition to the *Golden Legend*, for the latter relates that a single Angel commanded Heraclius to dismount and carry the Cross barefoot into the Holy City. The Bishop—probably Zacharias of Jerusalem, liberated by Heraclius from the Persians—occurs in the Tridentine revision of the *Roman Breviary*, and in a work that was constantly consulted by scholars for factual information: Flavio Biondo's *Historiarum ab inclinatione Romani imperii decades III*, written in the 1440s and later frequently printed.[12]

The narrative proceeds through the smaller panels to the larger central section (Plate 48 and Col. Plate II), a scene of greater complexity and grandeur than any other Elsheimer work. It is a synthesis of all influences that had shaped his style up to now: Dürer (whose *Feast of the Rosegarlands* was still in Venice when Elsheimer stayed there), Titian's *Adoration of the Trinity* ('La Gloria'), engraved by Cornelis Cort in 1566, Tintoretto's *Paradiso* and Rottenhammer's *All Saints* (Collection Earl Spencer). Yet he fused what he had learnt into a wholly arresting composition, with such attention to detail that the eye is constantly enchanted when scanning the multitude of figures without ever losing a sense of cohesion. Surprisingly enough, the *Coronation of the Virgin* does not take place centrally, as it does in the Tintoretto and Rottenhammer paintings just mentioned, but is placed at the upper left, hardly discernible to the eye. Although the elevated Cross is at the centre of the composition, it is towards the kneeling Virgin, received by the Trinity, that all the supporting groups converge like rays of light.

In no previous rendering of such a divine assembly were the individual members shown in such a tender and intimate relationship with each other. The high significance of the event is mirrored in the rich and colourful draperies and in an outwardly hieratic appearance of the participants. However, typically for Elsheimer, there is no idealization of the figures, who not only look but also act in the most ordinary way, while witnessing such an extraordinary event as the vision of the Cross. It was such rendering of religious or mythological scenes in terms of almost anecdotal realism—quite different from the more theatrical earthiness of Caravaggio—that so much appealed to Elsheimer's northern followers and imitators in Rome, who in their own works paved the way to an emphasis on the more narrative aspects of history painting in the Netherlands.

This ability to interpret a solemn theme without grandiloquence or sentimentality was already evident in *The Burning of Troy* and the stylistically related but more highly concentrated compositions like the *Judith* (Plate 36) and the moving little *Pietà* (Plate 42; left unfinished by the artist and overpainted in part by another hand). Even the somewhat more outwardly expressive *Three Marys at the Grave* (Plate 43), with—for Elsheimer—uncommonly rhetorical gestures, still conveys an intimacy and tenderness which flash, like a spark, from figure to figure and knit together the whole group like a cocoon. The atmosphere of

mystery is heightened by the luxuriant hanging vegetation of the cave in
miraculous event takes place. This very setting much appealed to some of t
followers, such as Jan Pynas (*Raising of Lazarus*, Plate 129) and especially Lastma
the painting was in fact once attributed. Interestingly enough, the *Three Marys* i
among the property of Paul Bril,[13] on whom its peculiar wild magic was not l(

Apart from some of the Venetian paintings and a few of the early Roman ones,
compositions concentrated on the single figure or on those themes which requir
presence of two or three main characters. But one composition among what m
sidered the 'middle period' works is the most spectacular of all his paintings:
(Plate 71). Already Sandrart acclaimed it as his masterpiece, when he saw it i
collection at Frankfurt, but it is doubtful whether he realized that it was left un
the artist and that most of the figures in the foreground had been overpainted an
by another, though probably contemporary, hand.[14] Nor was Sandrart aware of
of the rather puzzling incident depicted. It derives from an interpolated epis
Spanish picaresque novel *Guzman de Alfarache* by Mateo Alemán (1599), whicl
recently been translated into Italian, and which may have been suggested to the ar
of the many Spanish admirers of his work or by one of the members of the learne
which Elsheimer belonged. As is the case with all Elsheimer's works, there is no
whether it was a commission or was undertaken for his own pleasure.

The incident tells of Mercury's abduction of 'Content' at the behest of the jeal(
and of the attempt by the people to retain the goddess. The story can be traced bacl
Battista Alberti to classical sources (Lucian), and it is interesting to observe that in
of the two tapestries (the one covering the entrance of the temple, the other to th(
left) Elsheimer, in the figures of an emperor (on horseback in the centre; being cr(
the left), seems to have wanted to render in symbolic fashion temporal power, a:
to the divine one, personified by the presence of Jupiter. And as if to underline this
one can see the emblem of the Hapsburg double-eagle being held up in front of t
emperor on the extreme left—the same emblem which Hieronymus Bosch used wi
effect in the group of Emperor and Pope in *The Haywain*.

Il Contento is certainly Elsheimer's most extraordinary composition—basically :
The surging crowd's accented leftward movement is halted, so to speak, by Jupite
manding gesture of wrath on high. The background, separated from the foregro
by a window-opening, shows the self-indulgent, pleasure-seeking people whon
suspects of having abandoned the worship of himself. The movement here is in the
direction to that of the foreground. It is the compositional scheme which Lastman
for his *Paul and Barnabas at Lystra* (Plate 128; signed and dated 1614), a paintin;
Rembrandt copied in a drawing (Bayonne) and the Dutch poet Vondel celebrated in
It is the only composition by Elsheimer for which three preparatory drawings have s
(Plates 68–70), which show us how he must have gone about preparing some of h
elaborate designs. From an entry in his inventory it is clear that, like Tintoretto bef
Poussin after him, he had wax figures in his studio which he could move about like

on a stage.[15] Two of the drawings for *Il Contento* show the outlines incised for transfer. Normally such incisions indicate that the composition was to be used as a cartoon or for an engraving. In this case it can be seen that, as he shifted the wax figures around, he traced and retraced some of the figures from one sheet to another in various positions. In fact the drawing which comes nearest to the final design is almost wholly drawn with the stylus.

The accident of the painting having been left unfinished affords us an opportunity to gain a further insight into Elsheimer's working methods. The uncompleted figures in the middle distance were broadly sketched in, whereas the fully completed background and some of the figures in the foreground reveal how tightly he painted within strictly confined areas. He never swept his brush across large sequences of forms.

In spite of its incompleteness and additions, the painting makes an overwhelming impact both by its dramatic action and by the individualization of even the tiniest figures. The horrified faces of some of the onlookers—especially the two women with open mouths directly below Jupiter—are reminiscent, in their uncompromising and unexpected realism, of some of the figures in Luca della Robbia's *Cantoria*. To achieve on such a minute scale and with the finest technique (the copper was probably painted with a hairline brush under a magnifying glass) such moving details without sacrificing a strong overall impression is nothing short of miraculous and was no doubt the kind of work which made the Italian acclaim him as 'il diavolo per gli cose piccole'.[16] Although Elsheimer worked like a miniaturist and his paintings are wrought in the most delicate manner, his figures, if enlarged in the mind's eye, or photographically, will reveal a structure which can vie with any of Veronese's or Tintoretto's. He painted on a large scale within a small compass, and this was something which always elicited admiration.[17]

That a painting of the importance of *Il Contento* should have remained unfinished in the artist's studio at his death and tampered with by another hand shows how difficult it is to sort out his relatively small output into a coherent chronological sequence. He may well have taken up again some abandoned work at a later date. Not only is it impossible to assign definite dates to individual works—stylistic peculiarities and inspired guesswork are often the only guidelines—but always looking for neatly finished autograph works may mean embarking on a wild goose chase.

This problem is illustrated by a small, intimate work, like the *Pietà* (Plate 42), which from a photograph and reproduction has led many people astray in doubting its authenticity. It, too, was clearly left incomplete and was worked up by another hand. The division of hands is perfectly discernible in front of the original, which may well be the copper mentioned as the second item in the 1610 inventory (Doc. 12). It is basically an original Elsheimer, and the compassionate tenderness of the Virgin alone should make one pause before dismissing it. Some people have seen in it the influence of Annibale Carracci (probably thinking of the painting now at Naples), others the impact of Dürer. Yet essentially it is a highly personal rendering of a group that is set in less isolated surroundings. If one is reminded at all of another artist, it must be Michelangelo's sculpture in St. Peter's where—on a different scale and in a different medium—there is the same dignity and grandeur. Similarly, Caravaggio's

Entombment (Vatican Museum) has been cited in the case of Elsheimer's *Three Mar*
created at roughly the same time (1602–4), because the raised hands of the figur
occur in both paintings. But this is a gesture of lamentation which can be traced
as far as the High Renaissance and was probably familiar to both artists—for ex
an engraving by Mignon after drawings by Penni, Raphael's pupil.

There is, nevertheless, no denying that the *Three Maries* displays a rhetoric unc
Elsheimer, even if it is restrained compared with some of his contemporaries l
Yet even the exuberant Rubens was on occasion impressed by the more subdued
Elsheimer. *Judith and Holofernes* is a case in point (Plate 36). Here a scene of hor
down to an almost domestic calm, with dim candle-light casting a consoling gl
claustrophobic, windowless atmosphere, with the prominent still-life arrangen
table adding an almost comforting cosiness to the horrifying action. In such a
physical reflexes of the butchered commander attain an added power, which caug
Rubens's imagination (compare his own rendering of the scene in the engraving th
Galle made of a now lost painting; Plate 131) but also Rembrandt's (*Blinding*
Frankfurt); in fact it became almost a recipe for Baroque scenes of slaughter.

If Elsheimer's career had developed in a tidy sequence, with each new work
when the previous one had been completed, one might have suggested that after
the multifigured and comparatively dramatic subjects were set aside for more co
and restrained compositions, during the last two or three years of his life. And it w
been attractive to assume that what followed were the *Biblical Figures and Saints* (Pla
Col. Plate IV), today divided between Petworth and Montpellier.[18] However, *I*
very likely postdates the Italian translation of Alemán's novel (1606), whereas the
Montpellier series must at least to a large extent have been completed by 1605, the y
David Teniers the Elder, who demonstrably was so greatly influenced by some of t
cf. Plate 130), returned to his native Antwerp.[19] Nearly all the works by Teniers, a
a real pupil of Elsheimer, which are closest to the master's own paintings can be s
derive more or less from the backgrounds of the tiny Petworth/Montpellier panel
particularly striking in the case of the *Tobias* painting from this series; the precipito
fall, the broken tree-trunk across the river and the jungle-like vegetation were to
almost a signature of David Teniers. It is not surprising that the younger generation
should have fastened their attention on the backgrounds in these tiniest of panels—
calm, wide vistas, or nature at its wildest and most mysterious: they belong to t
miraculous details that Elsheimer ever achieved. The river landscape of the *St. Jo*
looks forward to Claude, to such an extent that we may wonder whether the young
knew the original, or perhaps Poelenburgh's copy after it (Pitti). The similarities betv
Petworth panel and Claude's *Pastoral Landscape* of 1638 (Plate 132) are striking inde
bird's-eye view of undulating hills (in *St. Peter*, *St. Paul* and *St. Lawrence*) and the
fantastic woodland scenery (*St. Anne with the Virgin*) set the pattern for nearly all the im
and gave rise to the prevalent notion of Elsheimer as a 'romantic' interpreter of
This misguided judgement has led to an erroneous picture of his work and to a f

incorrect attributions. The Petworth/Montpellier panels are the genuine works to use as a yardstick.

The monumentality of these figures ultimately derived from the series of Saints engraved by Schongauer and Dürer, which are on a comparable scale. For Elsheimer the Petworth/Montpellier figures are a kind of recall of his earlier German years, a rethinking of Dürer and Altdorfer, and it has been correctly observed that there is a resemblance between the figures in the Berlin altarpiece and the later Biblical figures. Yet a comparison between the two works demonstrates how much Elsheimer had matured in the intervening ten years. His development cannot be charted in a straight line, but proceeded in the form of a spiral. It might be said that with the *Biblical Figures* he had completed almost a circle, but emerged a level higher. Again, if the Petworth figures were enlarged, they would rival in monumentality those of the great Venetian and Roman masters. The landscape backgrounds, however, some with a high viewpoint, are a synthesis of the Venetian and Flemish traditions.

Another example of such a landscape is the Virgilian or Horatian *Aurora* (Plate 66). This is no longer background, but the chief carrier of the picture's content and on a scale more imposing than anything Elsheimer had hitherto attempted. The magical early morning sky, just touched by the rising sun, and the wide vista of the valley (reminiscent of the Anio, or the foot of the Sabine mountains) with the fortified building marking the middle distance, recession rendered by means of a diminishing scale of tones: this was a novel conception which Claude Lorrain understood. Whether the Braunschweig painting is wholly Elsheimer's original is questionable. There are many flaws: the whole of the left-hand side, with the two dimly discernible figures, has been overpainted to a degree which makes considered judgement difficult if not impossible. Scientific examination has revealed that the original figures were about twice as large as the ones now visible,[20] so that Holzinger's interpretation of the scene as the story of Cephalus and Procris may turn out to be untenable. It is interesting to note that it is exactly this controversial left-hand passage that Goudt omitted in his engraving of the composition. There are also superficially painted passages in the landscape, which lead one to speculate whether this was another of the works left unfinished by Elsheimer and interfered with by another hand—perhaps the hand of Goudt himself, for it has to be assumed that he owned the painting, from which he made his engraving in Holland in 1613.

If it is right to date the series of *Biblical Figures* and the *Aurora* to the middle of the decade, which is also the middle of Elsheimer's Roman career, these works can be seen as a kind of watershed. The elaborate compositions, containing numerous attendant figures, were being abandoned in favour of small groups or single figures, of which the Petworth series is an example. Less elaborate designs and greater emphasis on the narrative content and on the mood of the surroundings, all combine from now on to heighten the lyrical and human qualities of his biblical and mythological themes. Two paintings, *Tobias and the Angel* (Plate 72) and a rendering of the affecting climax to the story of *Apollo and Coronis* (Plate 76), belong to this new phase of Elsheimer's development.

The *Small Tobias* (Plate 72)—to distinguish it from a larger composition of the same theme —seems to have established Elsheimer's fame in Rome, if we can trust Sandrart's report. Its

appeal seems to have been instantaneous, for it was copied innumerable times
from the Book of Tobit had often been painted before, but what was novel—apa
catching details like the inevitable skipping dog and the frogs at the water's ed
relationship between the figures and the surrounding landscape, which is bathed i
golden light. The silhouettes of the two figures against the trees, the silhouettes
themselves—in a variety of hues—against each other and against the sky, and t
of the tiny figures and animals of the background in the water, all express pastor
beauty. But the popularity of the little painting may also have been aided by the
was the first of seven superb engravings made by Hendrick Goudt after Elsheimer
and widely disseminated. Goudt, a Dutchman who lived in the Elsheimer ho
several years, has to a large extent coloured—rather discoloured—the accounts of
life. He was an abrasive personality and will have to be discussed further later on.
graphic works by him have survived, and he made his début as a master print-r
the engraving of the *Small Tobias* (Plate 74), which is inscribed with the date 1
the few secure points in Elsheimer's work. Almost foreshadowing the chiaroscu
mezzotint, Goudt achieved in black and white the complete range of tone of t
colour. Which the original is, among the many versions that exist of this comp
been a matter of contention for some time. The version in the Historical M
Frankfurt, though damaged in parts, seems to be good enough to qualify, a
Elsheimer's technical hallmarks.

The *Large Tobias* was hardly less popular (Plate 89). This too, was engraved
some five years later (1613) when he had returned to Holland (Plate 90). Herc
etched an adaptation of the composition (from Goudt's print) and Rembrand
Segers's plate and reworked it, changing Tobias and the Angel into Mary and
their flight into Egypt and restoring Elsheimer's original *coulisse* of trees against
two figures were set and which Segers had omitted. Rembrandt's etching reinstate
action between landscape and figures which is such an important feature of F
composition. In Segers's version the figures appear somewhat unsupported, as if
Although Segers altered the aspect of the landscape background, the basic accents
expanse of undulating hills were retained, also by Rembrandt. The composition o
ground and middle distance of Elsheimer's design repeats to some extent that of
Tobias, in that the two figures are on one side of a little lake, with riders and cat
opposite bank. But in the *Large Tobias* we are on higher ground and the middl
consists of a densely wooded slope, beyond which—in melting recession—one sees
series of hills with a tower as the focal point. The arrangement is in fact an extens
landscape in the little *St. Lawrence* panel at Montpellier (Plate 63), but the scale of t
and the grand simplicity of the vision of nature go beyond anything Elsheimer had
hitherto. The little dog and the frogs have gone, and the focus is on Tobias tr
enormous fish along the ground behind him, with his guardian-angel by his side.
of protection are very evident in this foreground passage: the spread-out wings of t
the overhanging branches of the chestnut tree and elder bushes; and the still-life of

and poppies seem to halt the steps at the bank of the lake. That the composition makes such a strong impression is all the more astonishing since no version that can be accepted as an original has survived. Of the two paintings which have been seriously considered as possible originals, the one at Copenhagen comes nearer in style and feeling to Elsheimer's own period, whereas the one in the National Gallery, London (Plate 123), appears to be several decades later, especially in the summary treatment of the landscape, which is somewhat reminiscent of the copies that the younger David Teniers made after earlier painters.

If we read the sequence of Elsheimer's works correctly, it would have been about this period (c. 1606–7) that he turned for inspiration to Ovid's *Metamorphoses*, a copy of which was listed among his belongings at the time of his death. This anthology, in which mythological events and the forces of nature—indeed human and natural forms—often intermingle, was a world almost ready-made for an artist of Elsheimer's sensibility and lyrical imagination. Many artists before him had turned to Ovid for their subject matter, but few had brought to these scenes such expressiveness and eloquence, or such sympathy with the narrative. Every story, every figure—even the most exalted among the gods—is interpreted in unidealized, human terms, but the ordinary personages and their actions are transformed by the sublime poetic mood and mysterious atmosphere which pervade even the humblest detail.

In *Apollo and Coronis* (of which the best version, if not the master's original, is at Corsham Court; Plate 76) the shapes of the solemn yet luminous landscape seem to echo the movements of the actors in the great lament. Apollo has killed the pregnant Coronis because of her unfaithfulness, and the bare branches of the mighty tree overhang her pale dead body as if to protect it. In contrast, the luxurious foliage of the climbing plants along the tree trunk, intertwined with white and red roses, seems to reflect the white and red drapery on which she lies. The golden light from the left plays over the curves of the naked body and touches the richly embroidered collar to Apollo's cloak, as the remorseful god bends down to look for healing herbs to revive his beloved. Coronis—apart from *Venus*, the only female nude Elsheimer ever made the centre of one of his compositions—is unidealized, in conformity with that realism with which he interpreted all his themes, but the figure is transformed by the gentleness of the light upon it. This light also skims the highest tree-tops in the background—so alike to the two *Tobias* paintings—and touches the reflections of the trees in the pool. The dark hues of the bushes on the right are contrasted with the spray of sparks from the funeral pyre, which illuminate the active little group of mourning satyrs. It is the unifying element that light gives to the whole which transforms what might otherwise have been a naturalistic 'landscape with figures' into a poetic evocation, which has only ever been matched by Claude Lorrain. Even if Sandrart's description of Elsheimer's endless musings in front of nature is not to be taken too literally, there can be no doubt that the backgrounds to the Petworth/Montpellier figures, the two *Tobias* paintings and *Apollo and Coronis*, reveal an unusual awareness of natural forms and appearances and the response of a highly sensitive individual, infusing magic into quite humble subjects.

Magical in another sense might also be the word to describe *The Mocking of Ceres* (Plate 82), which is among the most imaginative of Elsheimer's inventions. Count Tessin, who owned

Goudt's engraving from it (Plate 86), did not know the subject and describ
catalogue as a 'sujet de sortilège'. This Ovidian theme seems to have occupied El
some time. He made various drawings and etchings (Plates 83–5), and possibly
paintings to judge from works which may well be copies after Elsheimer origina
deal with episodes of Ceres roaming the world in search of her daughter Proserp
ever, the scene which fascinated the artist most was the one in which Ceres arriv
with thirst, at the hut of an old woman and asks for a drink of water. The boy Stel
to see the greedy way she gulps the water, mocks her, and this infuriates the godde
that she transforms him into a lizard. Again there is the disadvantage of not k
original by Elsheimer of this composition. The version in the Prado (Plate 82), th
in Rubens's collection, cannot possibly be from Elsheimer's own hand, as it is far
ficially painted. Yet it is the best version we have at present. It varies in some detail
magnificent engraving which Goudt made in Rome in 1610, especially in the posi
boy's head. These discrepancies may well go back to Elsheimer himself, for a pain
composition on 'silvered' copper, begun and then abandoned, has recently com
which shows two alternative positions of the boy's head and three of his legs. Th
not easy to judge the uncompleted state of the panel, it is close both in size and st
Prado painting, and may possibly have been made in the studio when Elsheime
experimented with the alternative poses of the figures.

From the Prado painting and Goudt's engraving, it is at least possible to gauge th
of the original. No other figure in Elsheimer's work has the same imposing statue
like an antique sculpture, as this Ceres. With her face partly in shadow, the dynami
figure is expressed by the eager stride forward, as the water from the jug relieves th
throat, while the dramatic play of light from torch and candle throws into relief the
drapery and thus heightens the figure's monumentality. The composition must r
Caravaggio's *Conversion of Paul* as one of the most powerful images created in Roi
early seventeenth century. It contains details which are familiar from previous wo
hanging tendrils and the group in the background occur in similar manner in *A
Coronis*. But at least one figure was to reappear in a later work: the old woman, a m
wizened hag and benign matron, who—almost unchanged—takes the role of B
Jupiter and Mercury in the house of Philemon and Baucis (Plate 87). She is a cross betweer
woman at the foot of the steps in Titian's *Presentation of the Virgin* and 'Una valente
who appears at the end of Annibale Carracci's engraved *Cries of Bologna*. However, s
latter was only published in 1646, thirty-seven years after Annibale's death, any con
or influence—in either direction—must remain hypothetical. The painting could be
be Elsheimer's first true 'night piece'. It carries on from the earlier *Burning of Troy* a
on Malta, but the composition is more concentrated and the handling of light and d
far more subtle.

The 'night pieces' are not confined to outdoor subjects, and in fact the few interiors
Elsheimer's paintings could legitimately be included under this designation—all are
and artificially lit. No interiors are known after the few indoor scenes in the Berlin alta

and the *Judith*, until we come to the *Minerva* (Plate 78) and *Philemon and Baucis*, both obviously dating from the last years of his life. Hitherto the story of Jupiter and Mercury visiting the old couple Philemon and Baucis had always been set out of doors. In Elsheimer's painting, for the first time, it is depicted within the cramped confines of a domestic interior, whose details border on genre and look forward to Jacob Jordaens.

In spite of the unidealized appearance of the two gods, Rembrandt, who probably knew the work through Goudt's engraving, was sufficiently impressed by the figure of Jupiter to transform it into the Christ in his own *Supper at Emmaus* (Plate 135). In this connection it is interesting to note that there is in fact an analogy between the themes of Philemon and Baucis and the Supper at Emmaus: both deal with the revelation of the divine to mankind.[21]

The humble abode, with the barest necessities lovingly depicted, is reminiscent of the room with *The Annunciation* in the Berlin altarpiece (Plate 15). Again, the sources of light are a candle and two oil-lamps. These illuminate the crumpled bedding and Jupiter's cloak, which are the areas on which the light chiefly falls. Everything else appears at first veiled in a dim grey-brown tone. Yet gradually, as one looks more closely, the glow of various colours emerges: the wine-red and blue of the garments of both Jupiter and Baucis, and the yellow ochre of Mercury's vest, are contrasted with the duller grey-green of the distempered wall. The still-life of fish and vegetables in the lower right corner is not just picturesque adjunct, but hallowed by the light that falls on it. Light, as always with Elsheimer, is more than a mere agent in order to make the dark visible or to dramatize an event, as it is with Caravaggio. It seems as if the left-hand part of the composition is illuminated, not solely because this is where the oil lamp happens to throw a bright light, but because it is from there that the lives of the two old peasants—as they emerge from the dim, cluttered corner of their humble surroundings—are transformed by the presence of the two gods.

Goethe greatly admired Goudt's engraving of the painting, but he recognized, beyond the mystery of the subject, its inherent humour: Mercury is lolling undecorously on the bed, and behind him on the wall hangs a representation of his encounter with Argus, one of his less gallant exploits and the consequence of one of Jupiter's many amorous encounters. Rubens was so fascinated by the whole painting, and in particular by the figure of Baucis, that he incorporated her as one of the attendant women in an *Adoration of the Shepherds* (Edinburgh, National Gallery of Scotland).[22] The evident influence of Elsheimer's picture on Rubens's composition must have come from a knowledge of the original and not from the later print by Goudt (Plate 88), as the disposition of the interior of the barn and the direction of the light suggest, and therefore Elsheimer must have completed the work in Rome before October 1608, when Rubens returned to Antwerp.

Philemon and Baucis, like *The Annunciation* in the Berlin altarpiece and the *Judith*, is an almost claustrophobic scene. There is no indication of a window, closed or open. But the most confined and airless of all Elsheimer's interiors is the *Minerva* (Plate 78). This is one of three panels dealing with the realms of the three goddesses whom Paris judged: Juno, Venus and Minerva. The first is lost and is known only through Hollar's etching (Plate 79). The other two are in the Fitzwilliam Museum at Cambridge (Plates 77–8). In Hollar's time all

three panels were in the collection of Thomas Howard, Earl of Arundel. They
been intended as decorations for a cabinet or other piece of furniture. The three
reigning over their respective realms, represent the 'Vita Triplex', the three moc
the sensual, the active and the contemplative; Goltzius also engraved them like t
source which Elsheimer would probably have used was either an edition of
moralisé[24] or more likely Cartari's *Imagini delli Dei*, first published in 1556 and
repeatedly. On the other hand, as the members of Elsheimer's circle were much in
Stoicism, they may well have suggested to him a remoter source, Fulgentius th
grapher's *Fable of the Judgement of Paris*.[25] Both Fulgentius and Cartari interpret
goddesses and their spheres of influence in the same manner, and describe the attribu
are faithfully reflected in Elsheimer's three little panels.

In the *Minerva* (Plate 78) the only sources of light are once again oil lamps anc
with the addition of a faint glow from a brazier. All the modelling of the dimly d
figures is by the light falling on the faces and garments, a light that is almost over
by a shadowy darkness and hardly even reveals the actions of the protagonists.[26]
and his pupil are working in front of a model posed like a Marsyas; a geographer
replica of the Jupiter in *Philemon and Baucis*) examines a globe; and two scholars ber
folio. Seated apart from all this intense but silent activity, almost in isolation, is the
figure of Minerva (or Pallas, as the inscription in Hollar's etching reads) with hel
spear, resting one foot on a sphere, with the owl—her attribute—perched near the
This is Minerva as patroness of the arts but, far from being a commanding figure
brooding one, in pose and expression very like Dürer's *Melencolia*. The connection
melancholy, Saturn and the arts is of course well known. Like Elsheimer's early dra
the artist being presented to Mercury (Plate 24), the *Minerva* is very likely inte
express, by implication, the ardours and self-denial all creative work imposes on th
devote themselves to it.

The figure of Venus (Plate 77) resembles, even as far as the draperies on which
that of Coronis. Venus's realm is love, but also nature, in which Cupid with his b
roses and the satyrs and nymphs are preparing the celebrations for the goddess
libidinous feasts. It is interesting to compare the original in Cambridge with the cop
Academy in Vienna. Although superficially similar, the latter shows a far more perf
way of painting, noticeable in the features and the body of Venus and in the drapery
her. This applies also to the putto and the figures in the middle distance. These are th
of clue by which copies can be distinguished from originals. Furthermore, the clu
trees are reproduced more or less faithfully in the many gouaches which for so lon
borne Elsheimer's name but which must date from about forty or fifty years af
death.[27]

The matronly figure of Juno (Plate 79), seated with a sceptre, a tapestry behind
depicted as the patroness of trade and of those who seek worldly success. In the backg
in a hall somewhat reminiscent of Raphael's Villa Madama, men are seen carrying war
bartering with each other. It is conceivable that Elsheimer intended here to depict the i

of the Temple of Juno Moneta, which had once stood on the summit of the Capitoline Hill and which was also the Roman Mint.

It might be said that these three panels outline well the confines of Elsheimer's world. These confines were carefully circumscribed and were never exceeded; the sole exception is his *Self-portrait*. The other-worldly themes he chose had almost all been tackled by other artists, but he invested them with such a vivid sense of reality that each scene seems like a fragment of the everyday world, transformed by the artist's deep wonderment about it.

This transcendent realism can be seen at its most moving in the *Flight into Egypt* (Plate 91). Although it is impossible to be certain that this picture was indeed Elsheimer's last completed work (it has an inscribed date 1609 on the reverse), it must surely be considered the climax of his career. It is a masterly evocation of darkness and light. But it is also an essay in humanity and compassion that probably only Rembrandt, on a different scale and by different means, has ever equalled (Plate 136). The scene is lit by three sources: the moon and its reflection in the water, the pinewood-torch held by Joseph, and the sparkling fire fanned by the shepherds. These illuminate and thereby accent three distinct areas of the composition: the background, the main group of the Holy Family, and the left-hand side. An imaginative touch is the presence of the Milky Way and some of the more familiar constellations in the sky, creating an illusion of the vastness of the universe. It has been suggested that the elaborate rendering of the famous cluster of stars reflects the impact which Kepler and his theories (1609) and Galileo's observations (1610) had made, though an astronomer would spot many inaccuracies in the placing of the Milky Way and its relationship to the other stars.[28] The painting can be interpreted, beyond its immediate theme, as a demonstration of the unity between man and nature: nature reflecting the human situation. No other rendering of the Flight into Egypt conveys to quite the same extent the contrast between the fugitive Holy Family and the vast yet protective nature into which they have strayed, with the stars above and the promise of human contact with the group of shepherds round the fire, whom they are about to en-counter. Here is, as Goethe said about Claude to Eckermann (10 April 1829), 'highest truth, but no trace of reality'. The only contrast of colour, against the dark green of the trees and the subdued blue of the sky, is the red and dull yellow of Joseph's cloak. It is the light from the torch and the fire, as well as from the moon and its reflection in the water, that fills the otherwise almost monochrome painting with a magic that takes one's breath away. It is interesting to compare the way the source of light illuminates the Holy Family in Rubens's rendering of the subject (Plate 133) and in Elsheimer's painting, which no doubt initially inspired it. In the Rubens the light emanates from the Christ Child; in the Elsheimer it comes from a torch—a prosaic touch of realism, which however transforms the ordinary into the extraordinary. This would seem to be a paradox, seeing that Rubens had specifically chosen to emphasize the miraculous qualities of the Child, whereas, if one did not know the subject of Elsheimer's painting, the family might on the face of it appear like ordinary staffage figures. Yet it is exactly the virtual isolation of Rubens's group, with a tiny landscape backdrop filling in space, and led by two typical 'baroque' angels, which makes them look more

conventional than Elsheimer's more everyday group, united—it would seem—wi
the wide, glowing universe.

A *Flight into Egypt* was in Elsheimer's studio at the time of his death, and is the firs
listed in the inventory. It was obviously the most notable among the works left be
must have been specially described by Dr. Faber when he informed Rubens of El
death, for Rubens refers to it twice in the course of his famous reply, in which he o
help to the widow in trying to sell this work in Flanders, where at that time no v
Elsheimer existed. (See Doc. 18B.) Whether the painting to which Rubens referred
the one now in Munich and whether it is the same which Goudt owned and from
made his engraving, cannot be said with certainty.[29]

HENDRICK GOUDT AND OTHER FOLLOWERS

It was Hendrick Goudt (1573–1648) who was responsible for spreading Elsheimer's
the north through seven engravings of his works. The impact of these prints on fellov
many of whom had probably never seen any original by Elsheimer, can be det
numerous pictures, drawings and prints, and it may not be too far-fetched to sugg
even the young Samuel Palmer may have been moved by the intensity of Elsheimer'
of nature. The Elsheimer literature contains almost more about Goudt than on El
himself. But it is necessary to get a clear picture of him. Five years older than Elshei
was born in The Hague, where he probably received his initial training. Hardly any
known of his early work except a few drawings—skilful but uninspired—which ar
on the style of Jacques de Gheyn II (who had been in The Hague since 1598) and G
The style of Simon Frisius, with its broad hatching, is also akin to that of de Ghe
Goltzius, and it may be that Goudt collaborated with him or was supervised by him
paintings or prints are known of this period. In 1604 Goudt went to Rome and, acc
to the census records, lived in the Elsheimer household ('Henrico pictore') at least till
by the end of the following year he had moved to a house in a neighbouring street
Doc. 11.) He was given the Papal order of 'Conte Palatino a Cavaliere dello Speron d
This honour was fairly freely distributed at the time,[31] but Goudt was evidently very
of it, for he used it in his signature in all his prints.

The early sources seem to imply that Goudt was both Elsheimer's pupil and patror
that he kept the family solvent by accepting in lieu the bulk of Elsheimer's output. V
Elsheimer was unable to deliver his work in sufficient quantity and at a suitable speed, C
is said to have lost patience and to have had him thrown into the debtors' prison, where
supposed to have contracted his fatal illness. This story could only be verified if docui
were found to prove it. However, both Rubens's letter to Dr. Faber (Doc. 18) anc
contemporary account by Mancini (Sources, 2) imply that certain people had done Elshe
grievous harm, and had thereby hastened his death. However nefarious Goudt's conduct
have been, he did at least one great service to Elsheimer by his engravings. These are sc
thing of a miracle, for there are no graphic works extant from Goudt's hand that prepa
for these seven masterpieces, so that it seems as if he emerged fully armed as a master-engra

Two of the plates were made in Rome during Elsheimer's lifetime, and no doubt under his supervision: the *Small Tobias* (1608) and the *Mocking of Ceres* (1610)—both bearing Elsheimer's name as 'inventor' (Plates 74 and 86). The remainder were done in 1612 and 1613, after Goudt had returned to Holland, and in these five engravings he suppresses Elsheimer's name. It is thus more than likely that Goudt was in the possession of the originals from which he made his prints: the *Large Tobias, Aurora, Philemon and Baucis, The Flight into Egypt* and probably the tiny *Martyrdom of St. John*, the only print without a date (Plates 90, 67, 88, 92, 94). But this propagation of Elsheimer's work also had a somewhat sinister effect, for it is quite clear that Goudt in his own drawings—very much 'à la Elsheimer'—unconsciously or deliberately created a false image of Elsheimer's work, and especially of his drawings, an image that has persisted to this day. He certainly considered himself as Elsheimer's spiritual heir.

It is plain that in his own work Goudt lacked an original mind and had to feed on the imagination of others. From Elsheimer he took over motifs or whole compositions, just as Pierre Antoine Quillard rifled the work of Watteau. But even if Goudt was unimaginative, he had undoubted skill, as even his most undisciplined scribbles demonstrate. Like a parasite he fed on his 'host'. He became mentally deranged later in his life and one wonders whether signs of instability of character had not shown themselves already in Rome and whether this may have accounted for his ambivalent behaviour towards Elsheimer. He died in Utrecht in 1648.

In the Italian sources, Goudt is referred to as 'pittore', whilst in the Utrecht Academy of St. Luke he was registered as an engraver. Only one painting, a version of the *Philemon and Baucis* (Plate 134), has been attributed to him, though without any good evidence.[32] But there is a large group of drawings with a consistency of style which makes the attribution to Goudt very plausible. They show an undisciplined and even at times a violent streak and—as one would expect—an obvious lack of compositional invention, so that imitation and repetition prevail.

Whether Elsheimer ran a proper studio and had pupils working under him is not known. Some of the many surviving copies of his compositions seem certainly to be contemporary and they are of such high quality that one must surmise that they were painted directly under the eye of the master. The question of course arises whether some of the 'copies' are not really replicas from Elsheimer's own hand. However, what we know of his temperament makes it seem unlikely that he ever completed more than one version of a work. Lebrun, in his account of Elsheimer (1792), lists as copyists specifically Thoman von Hagelstein, David Teniers the Elder, Pieter van Laer and Goudt, yet it is impossible to assign any particular version of Elsheimer's compositions to any of these artists. Van Laer (if Lebrun was well informed) only arrived in Rome seventeen years after Elsheimer's death, but the others were certainly in Rome with Elsheimer, and so were Lastman and the Pynas brothers, from whose paintings a direct contact with Elsheimer can be deduced. To these must be added the Flemish artist Adriaen van Stalbemt, to judge from the paintings which can confidently be attributed to him (cf. Plate 113), although an Italian journey of his is not documented.[33] All

these artists came under the spell of Elsheimer, to such an extent that several of th
have at different times been attributed to Elsheimer himself. It was through such v
his style was passed on to the younger generation, a sort of Elsheimer at second ha
these artists transmitted were often rather superficial mannerisms: rocky landsc
ruined buildings, dark forests with lakes, luscious foliage interspersed with bl
flowers, heavily draped figures with a vague Old Testament air about them, often dra
lit. It was Rembrandt, above all, the pupil of both Lastman and Jacob Pynas, who
to see what lay behind. *The Rest on the Flight* (Dublin) and *The Supper at Emma*
already mentioned, to name only two works, are unmistakable and deeply moving
Rembrandt (Plates 135, 136); the recognition of an Elsheimer source in both of th
dawns gradually, so fully has it been assimilated. In both cases the derivations st
Goudt's engravings.

Whilst the above-mentioned artists were responsible for disseminating Elsheimer's
in the north, there were also northern artists in Rome who absorbed Elsheimer
interpretation of nature. Chief among them was Cornelis Poelenburgh, who came t
in 1617 and therefore did not meet Elsheimer himself. He made a number of copie
paintings, the best known being the series of *Biblical Figures*, now in the Pitti Gal
Plate 64). Following his example, Breenbergh and Agostino Tassi evolved the
Elsheimer-like landscapes, and through Tassi in turn Claude Lorrain learnt how to co
a landscape and evoke its special mood. Like Rembrandt, Claude was able to respond
deeper levels of Elsheimer's art. Claude's sense of the relationship between the figures
landscape they inhabit is so akin to Elsheimer's that one begins to wonder whether
not a far greater direct knowledge of his paintings than had hitherto been realized
Elsheimer's largely intimate utterance grew into a more elaborate language that was
stood by the best painters of the following generations.

PRINTS AND DRAWINGS

If Goudt can be considered Elsheimer's pupil, he cannot have learnt the art of print-m
from him. That Elsheimer did etch is confirmed by a passage in a letter from Rube
Pieter van Veen (Doc. 18C), in which he describes the method Elsheimer used to prep
white paste ground, typical of a man who is none too familiar with putting the etc
needle direct onto the dark resinous ground of the copperplate and needs to see clearly
he has drawn.[3] The few etchings (and the one very early engraving) convincingly att
ted to Elsheimer (Plates 4–6, 65, 75, 85, 96) bear out this inexperience. They are not v
that need detain one very long. As two of the etchings (*Small Tobias* and *Joseph and the C
Child*) (Plates 65, 75) repeat so closely his painted compositions, one wonders whe
Elsheimer had intended to disseminate some of his works to a wider public by such me
but then left it to Goudt, who succeeded brilliantly with his seven engravings. However,
bulk of the etchings which still go under Elsheimer's name are more likely to be by follow

The drawings are a different matter. More ink has been spilled on this controversial sub
than on any other connected with Elsheimer. When Bode first rehabilitated the artist at

end of the last century, he thought he could accept over three hundred original drawings by him. This number was gradually reduced by the subtraction of copies and imitations and original works by other artists, until Möhle (1966) arrived at just under seventy. Yet even this number, it is now clear, is too generous. It is only in recent years that a few drawings have been rediscovered which are directly related to known works and thus provide a clear standard for assessing Elsheimer's drawing style. These make it clear that, while he gradually developed a greater facility and assurance in drawing, the drawings never rival his paintings.

These preliminary drawings bear little resemblance to the majority of drawings to which Elsheimer's name has been attached over the years. The confusion was caused mainly by two groups of drawings: an album with pen sketches and a group of gouache drawings. The album, now dismembered, comprised 179 items and was acquired by the Städelsches Kunstinstitut at Frankfurt in 1868.[35] The inscription on the album stated (in Dutch) that the drawings were by Elsheimer. However, one of the sheets was found to have the address of Hendrick Goudt in Utrecht written on the back—a cuckoo in the nest—and Max J. Friedländer rightly warned that if one was by Goudt, there might be others. Gradually, more and more people came to realize that the majority of the drawings could not be by Elsheimer and were most likely by Goudt himself, imitating his master. Möhle finally retained seven as certain and another nine as doubtful in his catalogue of Elsheimer drawings. However, following Drost's (1933) tentative suggestions, Professor and Mrs. van Gelder came to the conclusion that none are by Elsheimer, but that all except two, by other artists, are altogether the work of Hendrick Goudt. Bode (1920) had already recognized that most of them depended on earlier sources, and the pen-work shows exactly the impatience and imitative tendency we have described.[36]

The other drawings which have misled people about Elsheimer as a draughtsman are the landscape-gouaches.[37] Möhle considered them 'to belong to the most secure part of his oeuvre' (p. 44), whereas in effect none of the attributions to Elsheimer can be traced back beyond the eighteenth century. Furthermore, the drawings can by no means be considered to form a coherent group from a single hand. Some of them are not even gouaches (Count Seilern's and that at Leningrad), others (Rennes) with farmhouses and the characteristic roofed haystack ('kapberg') are certainly Netherlandish, and some of these can be recognized as by Pieter de With (fl. 1650–60), a follower of Rembrandt.[38] And one of the finest (Edinburgh) bears the signature of the Rotterdam draughtsman Gerrit van Battem (c. 1636–84), also to be found on other authentic drawings by him. One might be inclined to group with it the gouaches at Paris, London and Berlin. Battem is now mainly known by his rather stridently coloured genre-scenes in gouache, but more subdued landscapes (Brussels, from the coll. de Grez) and religious compositions by him are also known. These are probably earlier works and suggest that he was a far more sensitive artist than has been supposed. The attributions to Battem and de With indicate that the majority of them must date from at least forty to fifty years *after* Elsheimer's death: that is to say c. 1650–60. As one fragmentary landscape-gouache (Möhle 66) is undoubtedly by Goudt, as the figure study on the verso proves, it might be asked if it was perhaps Goudt's example which provided the impulse for the whole

series. It takes more courage to dismiss these landscape drawings from Elsheim[
than to dismiss the drawings of the Frankfurt album. The quality of some of the t
the gouaches has led people to read into them an 'Elsheimer' mood, as if he l
seventeenth-century Samuel Palmer, and it is easy to understand how his name c
attached to them.

However, Elsheimer did indeed produce gouache drawings himself (Plates 73,
95), but these were chiefly figure subjects (Bathsheba, Ceres) and show all the cha[
of his modelling in the figures and draperies and his beautiful sense of the scale of [
in relation to the whole composition.

The handful of other drawings which can be attributed with confidence to El[
invariably in pen and ink—show an artist whom it is not difficult to associate with t
gouaches. The hesitant, sometimes awkward handling of the pen, evident in tl
drawings that have survived, remained with him throughout his career. That
preliminary studies for his compositions is proved by the *King of Bali* drawing (Pl[
the three surviving designs for *Il Contento* (Plates 68–70). Drawings of pure landscap
medium, have not come down to us and may never have existed.

CONCLUSION

Elsheimer was a complex personality, difficult to fathom. Contemporary accou[
Mander, Mancini, Baglione) all report that he was a strange character: friendly, ever[
ing and obsequious ('elcken in alles te gevalle', van Mander), but eccentric and wit[
Certainly in his Self-portrait he has a haunted look. Yet he was loved by his fri[
honoured by his fellow artists, many of whom—according to Mancini—accompa[
body to the grave. He was unable to produce a great deal, no doubt owing part[
painstaking methods—akin to that of a miniature painter—but also to a profound mel[
streak, which must have hindered his activity. Rubens, in his famous letter, called it
(indolence or lassitude), but it may have been a physical condition outside the artist's
But then Rubens, with his immense creative vitality, may not have made allowance[
quiet, contemplative mood that can be sensed at the root of all Elsheimer's composi[
may not have been so much 'accidia', but an uncompromising critical conscience t
each work, the desire to let it mature slowly and not to hasten its completion, that [
to produce little and often to abandon half-finished works. Such uncompleted par[
Il Contento and the little *Pietà*, and others are listed in the inventory. It is likely that his [
left with a mountain of debts and having to pawn some of the paintings,[39] had some c
'finished' by another hand in order to make them saleable. The question thus arises [
such hybrids can always be recognized for what they are, when one is searching for o[
works from Elsheimer's hand.

The answer must lie in the unmistakable grandeur and sensitivity of those paintin[
are wholly from Elsheimer's hand. It is easy to understand the deep impression his wo[
on the generations of artists that came after him. On the smallest scale imaginable for
painting, his inventions speak with such compelling force that not only a miniaturi[

IV *St. John the Baptist – St. John the Evangelist – St. Thomas Aquinas – Tobias and the Angel* (Cat. 17).
Petworth House (National Trust)

Hollar, but also Rubens, the great Baroque master of large-scale painting, fell under their spell. The designation 'painter–poet' is certainly justified, but not the romantic implication with which recent interpreters have invested the phrase. Elsheimer's feeling for nature, whether pastoral or dramatic, was new but it was never made the subject of a painting on its own, always as a foil for the human figure. His ability to render the appropriate 'mood' of nature, appropriate that is to the essence of the situation in which his figures found themselves, was inimitable and was only rivalled in later years by Claude Lorrain. His narrative skill was only matched by that of Rembrandt. But on the whole Rembrandt put few restraints on his emotions when relating a story. Elsheimer was a story-teller who had worked emotion out of his system, so that he could tell his story more clearly. He hardly needed to raise his voice even to relate the most momentous events. A great calm lies at the heart of his compositions, especially the later ones. Their impact stems from an inner spring of action and not from the outer skin of a theme. Elsheimer subdued his creative fires, and the finished works show little trace of the creative effort which no doubt went into them. Even if his oeuvre as a whole was comparatively small, its depth and range are great. He was most quiet and most self-effacing in his art—even Chardin spoke in somewhat louder tones. But his voice has always been heard by fellow artists and connoisseurs alike.

NOTES

1. Apart from the many hopeful, but obviously wrong, attributions among the works in British collections, one finds among the Elsheimer admirers at least one representative of the lunatic fringe: Mr. Shakespeare Hirst from Huddersfield, who in 1884 published a pamphlet entitled *The Life of Adam Elsheimer/Painter/Born at Frankfurt 1574/Died at Rome 1620/ Written & compiled by/Shakespeare Hirst/Owner of the celebrated Portrait/of the/Immortal William Shakespeare/Painted by the above Artist.* [The biographical data that follow are taken from Le Brun.] And in a later note: *Mr. Shakespeare Hirst has, besides the portrait of Shakespeare, two other large paintings, viz.: The Bacchanalian and The Martyrdom of Saint Sebastian, all of which are attested by the master's signature.*

2. *Innocence and Hope*, an allegorical drawing in the Museum Boymans–van Beuningen, Rotterdam (Inv. MB.255), signed: *Hans Rättnhamer von Minichen macht dises zu guetter gedechtnus Ano 1589 In Terffis* (i.e. Treviso).

3. A. Sagredo, *Sulle consorterie delle arti edificatorie in Venezia*, Venice 1856. See also M. Muraro, 'The Statutes of the Venetian "Arti" and the Mosaics of the Mascoli Chapel', in *Art Bulletin*, XLIII, 1961, p. 269, n. 27; 270.

4. Waddingham 1972, p. 601, fig. 14. As I have indicated (Andrews MJ 1973, p. 174, n. 21) the attribution to Elsheimer seems to me unfounded. It is very likely a work of collaboration between Rottenhammer and Bril, a suggestion which a comparison with the stylistically related paintings in Treviso would support, in spite of the much larger size and different support of the latter (see Note 6). The figures in all three works are very close indeed, and the landscape background in the Hampton Court painting is almost identical with those in the Treviso pictures. As I stated before, the clue as to who the artist of the Hampton Court picture might be, lies in the identification of the features of the bearded man in the extreme right-hand corner—obviously a self-portrait. This is certainly not the face of Elsheimer, as we know it from his *Self-portrait*, and no recorded portraits of Rottenhammer are known.

5. The copy in the Victoria and Albert Museum Library, for instance, has been marked and annotated by Francesco Trivellini, a painter from Bassano.

6. *Christ in the House of Martha and Mary* and *The Supper at Emmaus*, the first inscribed on the back: *1596 G a imitazione di Giacobo da Ponte dipinse, Paolo paesagio*. Canvas, 85.5 × 108 cm. Treviso, Mus...

7. See Doc. 4. D. Bodart, 'Les Tableaux de la Paul Bril', in *Mélanges d'archéologie et d'histoire au Professeur Jacques Lavalleye*, Louvain 1970 Inventory of the possessions of Dr. Johannes 1628), reprinted in W II, p. 210.

8. See the passage at the end of Faber's account *Mocking of Ceres* (Cat. 23) 'After he [Bril] foll manner . . .'.

9. Note the paintings by Bril, Jan Bruegel anc di mano di Adamo, con ornamento' (fol. 585v posthumous inventory). C. L. Frommel, *Frühwerk und der Cardinal Francesco del M dell'arte*, 9/10, 1971. It is further interesting Goudt's engraving after Elsheimer's *Mocking o* 1610) bears a dedication to Cardinal Scipio Bo

10. Bodart, op. cit., p. 13.

11. This is not the place to argue whether S landscape painter at all in any meaningful sense nor to put forward in any detail my belief th series of paintings were in fact designed by Saraceni the figures, and Jacob Pynas the ex scapes. This affects the importance of Jacob I Elsheimer.

12. The only other Bishop whom I have four with this scene is in Félibien's description of the n fresco-cycle by Daniele da Volterra in SS. Trini in Rome, which Elsheimer would have known. passage reads: 'Il [Heraclius] fut constraint de court à la porte de la Ville, n'étant pas en sa puissa un pas, & demeura ainsi sans passer outre, jusc *Patriarche Zacharie* lui donnant avis de quitte superbes dont il étoit revêtu, il se couvrit vêtement, & déchaussa ses souliers, pour m l'humilité de Notre Seigneur . . .' (A. Félibien, *les . . . plus excellens Peintres*, Paris 1666, Tom p. 241.) This, however, was a live Bishop, not

Elsheimer's panel. The answer *may* lie in one of two alternatives: (a) that the heavenly apparition is related to the tradition found in Theophanes's early ninth-century Byzantine *Chronographia* and elsewhere, that Zacharias died before the Cross was restored to Jerusalem. His dates as patriarch are given by modern authorities as 609–628/9, differing as to whether he died in Persian captivity or was liberated by Heraclius in 629. (b) that the Bishop is not Zacharias at all but a previous Bishop of Jerusalem, the martyred Quiriacus; he was originally a Jew called Judas and had pointed out to Helena the spot where the Cross was buried and he was later converted to Christianity and elevated to become Patriarch of Jerusalem. It is he who is shown standing next to Helena on the hill on the right in the *Digging for the Cross*. Possibly Elsheimer had intended to use this figure as the link between the two episodes as related in the *Golden Legend*. It might be worth drawing attention to Palma Giovane's depiction of the ensuing incident, *Heraclius's Entry into Jerusalem* (Venice, Gesuiti), in which a Bishop heads the procession behind the Emperor.

I am most grateful to Mr. D. F. Wright of the Department of Ecclesiastical History in the University of Edinburgh for taking so much trouble about this intricate problem.

13. Bodart, op. cit., pp. 11, 13, 14.

14. One may be forgiven for wondering, when reading Sandrart's account of this painting, with the great emphasis on the High Priest clad in white and the youths with sacrificial implements, whether he was in fact referring to the picture now in Edinburgh—it corresponds much more to Knüpfer's version of the same subject in Schwerin (Pl. 121), which however is clearly signed and dated.

15. Inventory of 1610, fol. 865r 'alcuni Modelli di cera di diverse figure' (Doc. 12).

16. Edward Norgate, *Miniatura, or the Art of Limning* (1650), ed. Martin Hardie, Oxford 1919, p. 43.

17. cf. Sir William Sanderson, *Graphice*, 1658, p. 19, where under the heading *Particular Masteries* he lists 'in little, Ellsamere'.

18. Eight of the series are at Petworth, one at Montpellier, but originally there must have been at least ten, possibly even thirteen. See Cat. 17.

19. For David Teniers the Elder, see vG-J I, p. 147; M. Waddingham in *Arte Illustrata* January 1970, p. 58; E. Duverger and H. Vlieghe, *David Teniers der Ältere*, Utrecht 1971; Waddingham's review of the latter in *Burlington Magazine*, February 1972, p. 96; Waddingham 1972, p. 605.
A *Preaching of St. John* in Leningrad (Inv. 6891), as 'Elsheimer Circle', hitherto ignored in David Teniers studies, is also likely to be by him.

20. Knut Nicolaus, 'Elsheimers "Aurora" im Lichte naturwissenschaftlicher Untersuchungen', in *Maltechnik/Restauro*, 1974, no. 2, p. 98.

21. W. Stechow, 'Myth of Philemon and Baucis in Art', in *Journal of the Warburg and Courtauld Institutes*, IV, 1941, p. 110.

22. In fact the figure in question has been partly cut off from the painting, and we only know of its existence through an engraving by Jan Witdoeck, and through copies after the picture.

23. The Middle Ages knew the distinction between the 'vita activa' and the 'vita contemplativa', to which the Renaissance (Marsilio Ficino) added the 'vita voluptuosa'. Lastman, in his inventory of 1632 (K. Freise, *Pieter Lastman*, 1911, p. 19) lists 'Drie tronien van [Frans] Badens [c. 1571–1621] als Venus, Juno en Pallas', and the inventory of the painter and picture-dealer Jan Snellinck (9–11 October 1638) lists under Nos. 82–84 'Dry panneelen van Venus, Juno ende Pallas, olieverve, sonder lysten', and under Nos. 123–125 'Noch 3 tronien van Juno, Pallas ende Venus, respective op panneel'. A. Monballien, 'Aantekeningen bij de Schilderijen-inventaris van het sterfhuis van Jan Snellinck (1549–1638)', in *Jaarboek 1976 Koninglijk Museum voor Schone Kunsten in Antwerpen*. These must have been separate panels and not a *Judgement of Paris* as Monballien maintains (pp. 258 and 260).

24. cf. Carla Lord, 'Three Manuscripts of "Ovide moralisé"', in *Art Bulletin*, LVII, no. 2, June 1975, p. 166.

25. I am grateful to Jennifer Montagu for references to Fulgentius.

26. On the significance of the colours in this panel, see Charles Parkhurst, 'Louis Savot's "Nova Antiqua" Colour Theory, 1609', in *Album Amicorum J. G. van Gelder*, 1973, p. 246.

27. See the passage on the gouaches, p. 41.

28. cf. Anna Ottani Cavina, 'Elsheimer and Galileo', in *Burlington Magazine*, March 1976, p. 139, and the author's reply to her arguments, *Burlington Magazine*, August 1976, p. 595.

29. See Cat. 26, and Andrews 1972, p. 597.

30. This is a suggestion made by Professor van Gelder.

31. For example Cigoli was made a Palatine Knight by Cardinal Scipio Borghese.

32. Coll. Wachtmeister, Wanås, Sweden (Pl. 134). Cf. H. Weizsäcker, 'Hendrick Goudt', in *Oud Holland*, XLV, 1928, p. 112.

33. See Andrews 1973, and Andrews MJ 1973.

34. Letter 19 June 1622. Doc. 18c.

35. The album ('Klebeband' or 'Skizzenband') was published by H. Weizsäcker, *Die Zeichnungen Adam Elsheimers im Skizzenband des Städelschen Kunstinstituts, Frankfurt a.M.,*

1923. Hitherto the album has only been traced back to the firm of C. G. Boerner in Leipzig, from whom Frankfurt acquired it in 1868. The first page bore the inscription 'D.42 Corbyn Barrow Lancaster 1848'. Barrow, a wool merchant in Lancaster, lived from 1803 to 1865, and Boerner's very likely bought the album at the sale of Barrow's possessions.

An English provenance is thus established. It should, however, be considered that it might be traced back even further, for in the sale of the belongings of the Scottish painter Andrew Geddes (1783–1844) *Catalogue of the valuable Collection of Pictures and Drawings*, etc. . . . *belonging to Andrew Geddes*, London (Christie) 8–14 April 1845, Lot 360 was 'A volume containing 107 pen sketches, by Adam Elsheimer, drawn with great freedom and effect' which was bought by H. Bohn, the antiquarian bookseller, for £7. Although there is a discrepancy in the number of items: 107 as against the 179 recorded in the Frankfurt album, it might be assumed that there had not been a miscalculation, but that the 179 sketches (some quite small) were stuck on to 107 pages, and that these, rather than the actual drawings, were counted in the Geddes catalogue. Whatever the answer is, it seems unlikely that there had ever been *two* albums, both with over 100 drawings, attributed to Elsheimer, so that it was possibly the Geddes volume that Corbyn Barrow acquired in 1845 or three years later.

Attention should also be drawn to an item in the inventory of Alexander Voet of Antwerp (6–10 Octob[e] lists 'Een boecxken van Elshamer' (J. Denucé, *Konstkamers*, etc. 1932, p. 325).

36. Yet in 1680 Goudt's own drawing-styl[e] recognized, for the inventory of Jan van Ca[p] an entry of two albums with drawings by G

37. The passage on the gouaches is based on the author at the meeting of the Association o at Glasgow in March 1976 (*Bulletin of the A Historians*, no. 3, London, October 1976, p.

38. See vG-J II, p. 35.

39. This becomes clear from the 'Quietati painter Ascanio Quercia (Carla Antonia's thi[r] his step-son, Elsheimer's son Giovanni Franc[e] which Quercia claims that he had to re[c] quadros ramineos [paintings on copper which his former wife was forced to pawn. Antonia died on 27 September 1620, and found in Archivio di Stato, 30 Not. Ca[p] Testamentum, 27 December 1619. She left h Quercia and half to 'Giov. Franc. Helshei See Docs. 15 and 16.

DOCUMENTS

Document 1: 1578. Record of Elsheimer's baptism.
Frankfurt, Standesamt. Drittes Kinderbuch, fol. 140—
Anthonius Elschamer schneider und Martta uxor ein sohn Adam hueb Adam Keck Apotecker zum Schwan.

Document 2: 1600. The first firm date of Elsheimer's presence in Rome.
Inscription in an *album amicorum* of Abel Prasch of Augsburg. (This Prasch was not the well-known organist from Augsburg, who had died in 1592. The Abel Prasch to whom Elsheimer dedicated his inscription was the second oldest son of the organist, who seems to have continued the album begun by his father.) Munich, Bayerisches Nationalmuseum, Bibl. 245 (MSS)
Mein Vertrauen Stet In Christo Allein
Zu Freundlicher Gedechtnus schrieb ich Adamus Ehlsheimer von Franckfurt dem Ehrenvesten und wolgelärtenn M. Abel Praschen Meinem günstigen Herrn und Gutten Freundt meiner in bestem zugedencken Actum Roma den 21 Aprilis Anno '600
The large gap between the heading and the rest of the inscription may indicate that Elsheimer intended to fill it with a drawing.

Document 3: 1606. Marriage contract between Elsheimer and Carola Antonia Stuart, 11 December 1606 (Andrews 1972, p. 598: Doc. I).

Document 4: 1606. Solemnization of the marriage. 22 December 1606.
Rome, Archivio del Vicariato: S. Lorenzo in Lucina, Matr. III 1590–1606, p. 165.
Die 22. xbris 1606
Dominus Adamus Eleshimer de Francoforti, et Dna Carl. Antonia pariter de Francoforti in Germania, degentes in nra Parrochia ad viam Paulinam contraxerunt matrimonium per verba de presenti iuxta forman S(acrae) R(omanae) E(cclesiae) et R^{dus} D. Franciscus Valletta C.R.M. Curatus eos coniunxit in eorum domo, presentibus testibus D. Doctore Joanne Fabro de Bamberga, et D. Pietro Facchetto Mantuano, et D. Paulo brilli de Anuersa.
A marginal note:
Hoc matrimonium fuit contractum in domo, ob licentiam R^{ssimi} Dom. Gipsij viceregentis propter infir^{tem} sponsae.
which shows that the ceremony took place at home, by special licence, because of the bride's illness.

Document 5: 1607. Census record of Elsheimer, his wife and Goudt, in the Via Bergamaschi.
Rome, Archivio del Vicariato. Stato d'anime, S. Lorenzo in Lucina. 1607. Bergamaschi
Sr. Adamo   *pictore*   *c*
Carla Antonia testuard moglie   *c*
Zerga famale fiamenga   *c*
Sr Henrico   *pictore*   *c*
Lucia d. Andrea mochi   *c*
The 'c' signifies that the person has been a communicant. 'Sr Henrico' refers to Hendrick Goudt. Who Zerga Famale was has not been established.

Document 6: 1607. Entry of a payment by Elsheimer in the list of members of the Accademia di S. Luca.
Rome, Accademia di S. Luca. Libro del Camarlengo de la Compagnia di S. Luca, congregatione de' pittori di Roma. Vol. II, 1593, etc. 1607, fol. 34
Adamo Egemieri—20 (bajocchi)

Document 7: 1608. Record of Baptism of Elsheimer's son Giovanni Francesco.
Rome, Archivio del Vicariato. Liber Baptismorum S. Lorenzo in Lucina. 1603–9, fol. 127 (October 1608)
Die 10.
Joannes Franciscus filius Dom. Adami Chellsmer ex Francofurto in Germania et Domae. Carolae Antoniae de Stuardae ex eadem patria uxoris eius, degentium in nostra parochia in via bergomensium, natus die 4. huius, baptizatus est a me Silvestro Ocono C.R.M. et susceptus a D. Joanne Fabro bambergensi germano et a D. Lavinia Ugolina Latina romana.

Document 8: 1609. Elsheimer's lease of an apartment in Rome. 9 February 1609.
Rome, Archivio di Stato, Collegio 30, Not. Capit. Officio 19, Not. Petrus Martinus Trucca, Instrumenta 1609, vol. 77, fols. 346r & v (for text see Andrews 1972, Doc. II, p. 599).

Document 9: 1609. Census record of Elsheimer and his family. Rome, Archivio del Vicariato. Stato d'anime. S. Lorenzo in Lucina. 1609
Paulina (i.e. Via Paolina)
Sr Adamo elshimus pictore   *c*
Carl. antonia moglie   *c*   *Giov. franc° i*
Sr. Henrico   *c*
Lucia mochi di prato serva   *c*

Document 10: Burial record of Elsheimer.
Rome, Archivio del Vicariato. Libro dei Morti II. S. Lorenzo
in Lucina. 1606–33.
Fol. 40.

> *Xbre 1610*
> *Adamo Pittore di francaforte germano morse alla strada Paolina,*
> *sep. in S. Lor. die 11.*

Document 11: 1610. Intimation of Elsheimer's widow to
draw up an inventory.
Rome, Archivio di Stato, Collegio 30, Notai Capitolini.
Officio 19. Not. Petrus Martinus Trucca, Instrumenta, 1610.
Vol. 82, fol. 863.

> *Secundo Curiae Capitolinae Collaterali*
>
> *Int[imatu]r omnibus infrascriptis p[raeten]sis, seu assertis*
> *creditoribus q. Adam Elzeimer Pictoris qualiter infrascripta*
> *Domina Instans creditrix dicti q. Adami et illius haereditatis*
> *occasione suae dotis ac donationis propter nuptias prout in*
> *Instrumento Rogato in actis infrascripti Notarii, aliisque iuribus*
> *etc. pro maiori suorum iurium conservatione et indemnitate, et*
> *ad omnem alium bonum finem et effectum etc. intendit describere,*
> *seu describi facere, seu inventariare res, et bona omnia quae-*
> *cumque etc. ad dictam haereditatem quomodolibet spectantia sine*
> *tamen praeiudicio omnium, et quorumcumque suorum iurium*
> *etc. Et talis descriptio, seu inventarium incipiet fieri die Dominico,*
> *que erit xix huius cum quatuor aliis diebus sequentibus, et*
> *amplius pro rerum exigentia singulis diebus de sero hora xx.*
> *Ideo ad illorum notitiam deducitur dicto nomine, et quatenus pro*
> *quocumque eorum praetenso iure, et interesse deducendum esset,*
> *seu citandi venirent, et non alias et cetera, ad effectum ut possint*
> *intervenire quatenus velint dictae descriptioni, seu inventario etc.*
> *Instante Domina Carola Antonia Astuarda uxore relicta di q.*
> *Adami predicti.*
> *Do. Petrus Martinus Trucca est notarius.*
> *Ill.Do. Henrico Goudt, in hospitio ad signum Ducis Parmae in*
> *via Crucis nuncupata*
> *—Dmo Paulo Brillo Pictori e conspectu Collegii Graecorum*
> *—Dmo Marcello Lopes Sutori in Via Bancorum e conspectu*
> *Vici nuncupati della Pall . . .*
> *—Dmo Henrico (★★★★) Aromatario apud Turrim Nonae.*
> *—Dmo Paulo (★★★★) Banderario apud Horologium Card[ina]*
> *lis Sfortiae [. . . . .] die XVII xbris 1610*

Document 12: 1610. The Inventory.
Rome, Archivio di Stato. Collegio 30, Notai Capitolini,
Officio 19. Not. Petrus Martinus Trucca. 1610. Vol. 82,
fols. 861–2 and 865–6. (Fols. 864r & v are blank.)

Fol. 861r.

> *Die Decima nona mensis decembris 1610 Inventarium*
>
> *Hoc est Inventarium omnium, et singulorum bonorum et*
> *rerum repertor[um]. In Domo, ubi habitabat q. D. Adam*
> *Elszeimer francoforten[sis] Pictor dum vixit in Urbe posita*
> *Romae in Reg.ne Campi Martis In via Paulina iuxta sua*
> *notissima latera factum ad Instantiam, Ill[mo] D. Carolae*
> *Antoniae Astuardae de Francoforte relictae dicti q. Adami, cum*
> *protestationibus tamen, et declarationibus in fine presentis*
> *Inventarii specificandis et describendis, quae bona sunt Infrascripta*
> *videlicet.*

> *Nella Camera dove d° q. Adamo dor...*
> *In primis Un quadro In Rame, di grandezz...*
> *mezzo Incirca dipintovi la M[adonna] (crossed...*
> *et S. Gioseffe quando vanno in Egitto, con G...*
> *figliolo, corniciato di legname di pero nero co...*
> *attorno.*
> *Un quadretto In Rame della Pieta cornici...*
> *alquanto vecchio.*
> *Un Rame abozzato di prospettiva dove dove...*
> *di S. Pietro quando negò Gesu Christo Nost...*
> *Un Rame dove è dipinto Il dio del Contento ...*
> *non finito.*
> *Doi Rametti piccoli d'una istessa grandezza q...*
> *non finito.*

Fol. 861v.

> *Un Rame d'un palmo et mezzo in circa di ...*
> *solamente.*
> *Un altro Rame di paese similmente abozzato so...*
> *Quattro Rami uno più piccolo dell' altri abozzat...*
> *si conosce che sia.*
> *Una Cornicetta Indorata con tutti li sop[ra]d[ett...*
> *mano del d° q.Adamo.*
> *Un quadro della Mad[on]na Con Christo In...*
> *corniciato, et indorto, di pittura ordinaria.*
> *Un quadro grande di S. Franc[esc]o in tela di p...*
> *senza cornice.*
> *Un quadro della Natività di N.S. Gesu Christo...*
> *Un letto di noce con le colonne alquanto ina...*
> *matarazzi di lana,*
> *Un pagliariccio et doi coperte di lana ord[ina]rie ...*
> *Un fortiere coperto di pelle rossa.*
> *Una Cassa d'albuccio corniciata di noce*
> *Doi tavolini piccoli con le loro piedi à telaro*
> *Doi Scabelli dipinti verdi vecchi*
> *Doi cassette da servitio delle quali una depinta e ...*
> *Una Cunna da putti piccola ordinaria*
> *Un specchio grande de Christallo con cornici Indo...*
> *Cinq. lenzola grandi grosse usate*
> *Doi altre para di lenzola piccole similm[en]te gros...*
> *Cinq. Camise da homo, delle quali doi ne sono bo...*
> *Vinti cinq. salviette grosse usate*
> *Otto Canavacci usati*
> *Un Cortinaggio di tela rigata mezzo rotto.*

Fol. 862r.

> *Cinq. tovaglie usate tra le quali ve ne è una sottile...*
> *Un paro de Capofochi di ferro con le palle d'ottone...*
> *Una graticola di ferro; molle et paletta di ferro: U...*
> *In una Cassettina vi sono le infr[ascritt]e robbe cioè ...*
> *di pegno dato per scudi venti sopra un padig...*
> *indenne et una zimarra di raso nero stampato, la ...*
> *se dice esser della d° Sig. Carola Antonia impe...*
> *sop[radet]to Padig[lio]ne a Crescentio Frascati he...*
> *Un altro bolletino di tre lenzola, et un anello d'oro à...*
> *della d° Sig[no]ra Carola Ant[oni]a impegnate ...*
> *per scudi 5.*
> *Un altro bollettino d'un vezzo di perle de n[...*
> *impegnate al d[ett]o hebreo per scudi venti di m[o...*
> *Un' altro bollettino d'un ferraiolo di seta drappata ner...*
> *al sopradetto hebreo per scudi sette di m[one]ta.*

Cinq. sedie di paglia da donna

Un vestito di velluto usato, cioè calzoni et casacca, et un-
ferraiolo di panno usato bene disse esser in mano delli preti di
S. Lorenzo in Lucina per pegno seu a tanto, che a lor fusse
stato pagato il Sotterratorio et altro che li viene per sopellire
il d° q. Adamo.

Una spada ordinaria vecchia.

Un libro de l'historie et antichità giudaiche di Gioseffe Hebreo.

Un Decameron del Bocaccio.

Fol. 862v.

Un quadro d'un Crocefisso con il suo taffettà verde con li
merletti d'oro.

Nella Cucina

Un letto di banchi et tavole vecchio con un pagliariccio, un
matarazzo grande et uno piccolo con le colonne bianche vecchio.

Una coperta di lana verde tarlata

Una coperta di taffettà verde foderata di tele gialla rotta, et
magnata da sorci

Un quadretto in tela di S. Francesco et S. Antonio

Un altro quadro di S. Geronimo senza telaro

Un quadro in un telaro d'una Madd. et Gesu Christo abbozzato.

Una tavola ordinaria da Cocina et un tavolino piccolo d'antano.

Quattro Candellieri d'ottone usati

Una lucerba d'ottone da olio a gguisa di Candelliere

Una [. . .] grande di rame

Un Caldaro di rame mezzano comp[rato] per prezzo di doi scudi

Un altro caldaro di rame piccolo

Una Padella; Un bolzonetto di rame; una grattacascio

Un Cappello di feltro berettino con il cordone nero

Un Ingegno di legno da tornire

Una sedia di legno alla Pistolese

Un mortaro di marmo piccolo con il suo pistone

Una padellina piccola di rame, Una fiasco di Stagno

Un cortello da Cocina grande; Un buzico di terra da olio

Diversi piatti, et pignatte piccole et grandi di poca valuta

Un tre piede di ferro ordinario per caldari; Un tondo di stagno
usato.

Fol. 865r.

Un bicchieri di stagno usato; Un scaldaletto vecchio senza manico

Un colletto vecchio

Doi secchi di Rame al pozzo con un pezzo di catena per
ciascuno et la loro corda.

Un Carriola di legno, Un rinfriescatoro di Rame

Un cavaletto di legno per dipingere, Un pagliariccio piccolo
vecchio

Sei libre accia filata di stoppa et lino in matasse

Un secchietto piccolino di rame; Un telaro d'un paese veccio

Un Mantello piccolo

Nella Camera della Serva

Un letto cioè banchi e tavole pagliariccio et una cop[er]ta vecchia
di lana

Doi telari vecchi, Un carratello da tener l'aceto

Nella stanza dove lavorava il d° Adamo

Tre quadri delle stagioni abozzati in tela senza cornici

Un Ecce homo abozzato in tela; Doi quadri di doi donne

Una Santa Caterina abozzato in un quadro di tela

Un Christo nel l'horto in tela abozzato

Un quatro abozzato in tela piccolo di S. Giovanni; Un Tobia
in tela abozzato

Diverse carte stampate di poco prezzo in una cassa vecchia, et
per le mura di d° stanza alcuni Modelli di cera di diverse
figure; Doi Cavalletti da dipingere

Una cassa vecchia dipinta verde

Un fortiere coperto di pelle rossa, con dentro un quadretto in
carta pecora abozzato

Doi fondi di scatole con diverse sorte di colori, di poca quantita
per sorte

Un paro di tenaglie di ferro piccole; Un libro de diversi disegni,
et alcune stampe d'architettura; Doi altri libri uno della
metamorfose d'ovidio, et l'altro che tratta della pittura dell'
Alberti, un altro libretto del trinciante,★ et altra carte [. .]

Una scala di legno; Un par de stivali bianchi, et un par de
speroni

Un banco di legno d'olmo; quattro telari d'antano longhi,

Un altro paro di tenaglie ord[ina]rie. Un Ancudinetta di ferro
in un ceppo

Doi seghe, diversi altri ferretti tra lime et altri; Un pianelletto
piccolo

Fol. 865v.

Un trapano con il piombo; Un pezzo di tela turchina

Nella Saletta

Corami vecchi di poco prezzo delli quali è parata d° saletta

Un quadro in tela d'una Lucretia Romana; Un altro simile del
ritratto del d° q. Adamo

Un altro quadro di Christo nel horto; Tre teste di tre papi, cioè
di Paolo quinto et Paolo terzo et Gregorio decimo quarto tutte
senza cornici

Una testa del beato filippo neri in tela senza cornici; Un
quadretto piccolo d'una Madalena senza cornici; Un quadro
in tela abozzato grande

Un quadro longo in tela di S. Barbara; Una testa del Card[ina]l
Baronio in tela

Un quadro con la Mad[onn]a con Christo, et S. Giovanni in tela
con cornici nere

Un quadro corniciato di S. franc[esc]o, doi ritratti piccolo
corniciati

Una Canna d'albuccio tinta di color di noce; Cinq Scabelli
dipinti verdi con un altro simile; Doi sedie vecchie; Un
travolino di noce con suoi piedi; e cassetta

Una credenza vecchia con tre cortelli da tavola et una forchetta;
Un paro di Capofochi d'ottone con una gabbia da ucelli di fil
di ferro.

Nella cantina

Una carratello voto una tinozza da fari la boccada; Una vettina
piccola di terra

Una Mezza botte vecchia etc.

Una patente de quattro lochi del Monte delle Cancellarie
vacabile hora ridotti à non vacabili a favore della d° Sig[no]ra
Carola Ant[oni]a q[ua]li disse essere di quelli che lei dette in
dote al d° q. Adamo.

Quae omnia bona ut s[upr]a Inventariata cum protestat[ation]ibus
et reservationibus infr[ascript]is et sine praeiud[icion]e huius
dotis, donationis propter nuptias et aliorum suorum iurium
dotalium quorumcunque d[ta] D. Carola Antonia retinuit penes se
ut latius infra dicetur [. . .]. Quae D. Carola Antonia Astuarda
sup[ta] Bona (exceptis illis picturis ereis manu d[i] q. Adami) sint ut

---

★ V. Cervio, Il Trinciante, Venice 1581 and Rome, 1593.

asseruit ex illis bonis d⁰ suo viro In dotem traditis quorum
Dominium ipso Jure mortuo Marito, ad uxorem revertitur,
Verum, quia dᵃ bona sunt maxime deteriorata, et multa ex eis
(Fol. 866r) deficiunt ut ass[eru]it, et ad complementum scutorum
mille m[one]tae ipsi Adamo per ipsam D. Carolam Antoniam
in dotem solutorum prout constare dixit in Instrumento dotali
in actis meis rogato die undecima Decembris 1606 seu et cetera,
ad quod et cetera, et aliorum scutorum ducentorum quinquag[in]ta
de m[one]ta pro quarto dotali iuxta formam statutor[um] Urbis
superlucratis(?) comprehensis etiam pretio, et valore dictarum
picturarum manu di q. Adami factarum minime sufficiant.
Volens tamen hac In re suae indemnitati, et conservationi
suae dotis aliorumq. suorum Jurium omnium praedictorum
occurrere, et ad omne alium bonum finem, et effectum, In-
timatis prius pretensis Creditoribus dicti q. Adami per S[anctissi]-
me D.N. Papae Cursorem prout In folio quod mihi Notario
et cetera tradidit tenoris etc., Die et Hora Intimatis confecit,
confecique fecit per me Notarium et cetera huiusmodi In-
ventarium modo quo supra cum protestatione praedicta et
Infrascripta ulterius quod, quae non sunt apponenda habeatur
prout haberi voluit, pro non appositis et salvo semper Jure
addendi, et minuendi et sine praeiudicio quorumcumque
suorum Jurium, sibi quomodolibet competen[tium] et com-
petiturorum, ac etiam non declaratorum infrascripta, quod intendit
dᵃ bona retinere in posterum non amplius retinere Jure familiari-
tatis sed pro suis Juribus dotalibus praedictis et aliis quibuscunque
cum reservatione etiam expressa, quod omne, et totum id, quod
deficiet seu deficere apparebit pro complemento dictae summae
scutorum 1250 intendit omnino, a quocunque herede vel heredibus,
et bonorum omnium etc. hereditatis dicti q. Adami, et ad illam
quomodolibet spectantibus et pertinentibus detentoribus, et
possessoribus exigere, recuperare, repetere, consequi et rehabere,
una cum multis expensis factis funere dⁱ q. Adami et aliis debitis
per dᵗᵘᵐ q. Adamum relictis, et per ipsam D. Carolam Antoniams
solutis, et forsan soluendis in futurum; Ita ut in nihilo sibi per
huiusmodi Inventarium et declarationem nec etiam In minimo
praeiudicatum censeatur, et ita dixit reservavit (Fol. 866v)
declaravit et protestata fuit non solum praemisso sed etiam omni
alio meliori modo et cetera, super quibus et cetera.

Actum Romae In Regione Campi Martii in superscripta Domo
ut supra posita et confinata, presentibus Mag.ro D. Thoma
Latino florentino et D. Virgilio de Salvis fulginatensi Caldarario
In Urbe testibus.

NB: It cannot be assumed that all the paintings were from
Elsheimer's own hand. The marriage contract stated that the
wife was bringing into the household "quadris ac bonis
mobilibus", which may have been by her first husband.
However, we have the assurance that the first nine items
listed are paintings by Elsheimer's own hand (Fol. 861v,
line 4: ". . . tutti li sopradetti rami fatti di mano del d° q
Adamo"), and "picturis ereis manu di q Adami" are referred
to in the postscript.

Document 13: 1611. Marriage contract between Ascanio
Quercia and Carla Antonia Astuarda.
Rome, Archivio di Stato. 30 Not. Capit. Officio 19. Not.
Tranquillo Pizzuto. Vol. 85, fols. 380 r & v and 387.
16 October 1611.

Document 14: 1612–19. Summaries of the co
between the Grand Duke of Tuscany in Flo
representatives in Rome, regarding the altar
the True Cross. (Full text in W II, pp. 204–8.)
Archivio di Stato di Firenze, Fondo Mediceo (
(a) FM 3506. 25 August 1612. The painter A
writes from prison in Rome to the Ducal Cour
town that he has seen in the house of a Spaniar
ings on copper by Adamo Tedesco on the story
and a 'Paradiso', which he advises the Grand
as otherwise the owner may offer them to his ov

    The same sheet contains—under the date
1612—an order to write to Guicciardini, the T
sador in Rome, to look at the paintings with Lo
and give an opinion.
(b) FM 3506. 8 September 1612. Lorenzo Usin
the Secretaries, writes to Tassi, asking him to
with the Tuscan ambassador in Rome.
(c) FM 3506. 26 September 1612. Tassi writes tc
(Giov. Perez) and asks him to show the
Guicciardini. He also mentions his quarrel
Gentileschi (whose daughter he had raped) an
Spaniard's intervention to release the painter fr
cell in the Corte Savella.
(d) FM 3327. 5 October 1612. Guicciardini s
sketch of the altarpiece and quotes Cigoli's op
work is not worthy to enter the Grand Duke'.

    (A more careful sketch of the frame and an
tion of the seven panels is given on anoth
Miscellanea Medicea F.93 c.192—on which the
Pl. 47 is based.)
(e) FM 3506. 8 October 1612. Belisario Vinta
Guicciardini's report and has forwarded it
(f) FM 3334. 4 December 1619. Guicciardini
Grand Duke to say that the Spaniard is in finan
and would be satisfied with less than the three t
he originally asked 'for the most beautiful
Adamo has ever made'. As the ambassador d
his own judgement, though the painter Giorչ
expressed himself favourably about the painti
to be allowed to ask the opinion of the Cardiᴦ
(Followed by an exact description of each pan
(g) FM 3334. Letter from Andrea Cioli to Cu
approving this arrangement.
(h) FM 3514. 10 December 1619. Order fron
Guicciardini.
(i) FM 3334. 14 December 1619. Guicciardini
purchase, with the support of the Cardinal d₀
the 'reliquario' is sent to Florence on 28 Decₑ

Document 15: 1619. Testament of Carla An
27 December 1619.
Rome, Archivio di Stato. 30 Not. Capit
Testamentum.

Document 16: 1620. Burial record of Carla ⸗
Archivio del Vicariato. Libro dei Morti. S
Lucina. Fol. 107. 1620.
    Settembre
    Carl. Antonia Testarda de . . . moglie d'Asc

*morse alla strada Paulina, sept. in la chiesa della Santissima
Trinità de Monti a di 27.*

Document 17: 1629. 'Quietatio' between Ascanio Quercia
and Joannes Francesco Helsemer [*sic*].
Rome, Archivio di Stato. Collegio 30. Not. Capit. Officio 19.
Not. Tranquillo Pizzuto. Vol. 153, fols. 542–3 and 550–1.
Quercia renounces all claims upon Giovanni for the sums
he has paid under his guardianship and for the debts of his
father [i.e. Adam Elsheimer] and that of his mother,
including 44 scudi for redeeming some paintings on copper
[nonullos quadros ramineos] pawned by Carola Antonia.
And Giovanni, wanting to enter the order of St. Benedict
renounces all claims upon Ascanio and cedes all his property
to him.

Document 18: Extracts from the letters of Peter Paul
Rubens (quoted from the edition translated by Ruth
Saunders Magurn. Cambridge, Mass., 1955).

(a) *To Johann Faber*   *Antwerp, April 10, 1609*

Most Illustrious and Excellent Sir:
. . . I beg that on the arrival of Signor Scioppius in Rome you will
commend me to him, and to his convert, Signor Adam, to Signor
Enrico and to the other friends whose good conversation makes me
often long for Rome. Patience: non cuivis homini contingit ea.
[This does not fall to every man-Horace Epistles 1.17.36]
I kiss your hands with all my heart, and so does my brother, who
tells me that he wishes to serve you likewise, when his Juno gives
him permission. Vale.

> *Your most affectionate servant,*
> *Peter Paul Rubens*

(b) *To Johann Faber*   *Antwerp, January 14, 1611*
My Illustrious and Honored Sir:
I have received from you two letters of very different tenor and
content. The first was thoroughly amusing and gay; but the second,
of December 18, was the bearer of the most cruel news—that of the
death of our beloved Signor Adam,—which was very bitter to me.
Surely, after such a loss, our entire profession ought to clothe itself
in mourning. It will not easily succeed in replacing him; in my
opinion he had no equal in small figures, in Landscapes, and in
many other subjects. He has died in the flower of his studies, and
adhuc sua messis in herba erat. [(His wheat was still in the blade
(Ovid, Heroides 17.263)]. One could have expected of him res
nunquam visae nunquam videndae; in summa ostenderunt terris
hunc tantum fata. [(Things that one has never seen and never
will see; in short, destiny had only shown him to the world
(cf. Aeneid 6.869)].

For myself, I have never felt my heart more profoundly pierced by
grief than at this news, and I shall never regard with a friendly eye
those who have brought him to so miserable an end. I pray that
God will forgive Signor Adam his sin of sloth, by which he has
deprived the world of the most beautiful things, caused himself
much misery, and finally, I believe, reduced himself to despair;
whereas with his own hands he could have built up a great fortune
and made himself respected by all the world.
But let us cease these laments. I am sorry that in these parts we
have not a single one of his works. I should like to have that
picture on copper (of which you write) of the "Flight of Our Lady
into Egypt" come into the hands of one of my compatriots who
might bring it to this country, but I fear that the high price of
300 crowns may prevent it. Nevertheless, if his widow cannot sell
it promptly in Italy, I should not dissuade her from sending it to
Flanders, where there are many art-lovers, although I shouldn't
want to assure her of obtaining this sum. I shall certainly be willing
to employ all my efforts in her service, as a tribute to the dear
memory of Signor Adam. And with this I kiss your hands with all
affection, and also on behalf of my brother. He is greatly surprised
at the delay of his letter to Signor Scioppius, who could be classed
among the antiquities of Rome, were he not known as a modern
author. I'd write also something on the doings of Don Alfonso and
Martellano, but that his subject seems little suited to the tragedy of
Signor Adam, which merits an entire letter a qua exulent risus
jocusque [from which jokes and pleasantries be banished].
Again I commend myself to your good graces, praying heaven to
grant you every happiness.

> *Your most affectionate servant,*
> *Peter Paul Rubens*

Surely the widow would do well to send that picture on copper (the
Flight into Egypt) directly to Antwerp, where there are countless
numbers of people interested in works of small size. I shall take
particular care of it and serve as curator with all my ability. And
if the painting should not be sold immediately, we shall in the
meantime find a way to advance her a good sum of money on it,
without prejudice to the sale.

(c) *To Pieter van Veen*   *Antwerp, June 19, 1622*
Most Illustrious and Honored Sir:
. . . I am glad that you have found that method of drawing on copper,
on a white ground, as Adam Elsheimer used to do. [In margin:
As I imagine, but perhaps you have a still better method than that.]
Before he etched the plate with acid, he covered it with a white
paste. Then when he engraved with the needle through to the
copper, which is somewhat reddish by nature, it seemed like drawing
with a red chalk on white paper. I do not remember the ingredients
of this paste, although he very kindly told me.

> *Your affectionate servant,*
> *Peter Paul Rubens*

MAIN SOURCES

1. *Carel van Mander, Het Leven der Doorluchtighe Neder-landtsche en Hooghduytsche Schilders.* Haarlem 1604 (though the 'privilegie' is dated 19 July 1603!)

> *Daer is noch teghenwoordigh te Room een uytnemende Hooghduytsch Schilder, Adam gheheeten, gheboren tot Franck-foort, wesende een Cleermaeckers oft Snijders soon, welcken in Italien comende, was noch redelijck slecht, maer is te Room wonderlijck toghenomen, en door wercken een constigh werckman gheworden: doch begheeft hem niet besonders te teyckenen: maer sit in Kercken oft elder de dingen der fraeye Meesters stadigh en besiet, en druckt alles vast in zijn ghedacht. Hy is wonderlijken aerdigh in te schilderen fraey inventien op coper platë, hoewel hy niet veel en werckt, dan is wonder veerdig. Hy is heel goelijcx, en elcken gheern in alles te gevalle, wesende dit Jaer 1604. ontrent 28. oft 30. Jaren oudt.*

Translation.

At the moment there still lives in Rome an excellent German painter called Adam, who was born in Frankfurt, the son of a tailor. When he came to Italy his skill in painting was still rather poor, but in Rome he made amazing progress and through hard work became a skilled craftsman. He does not busy himself particularly with drawing, but rather sits in churches or elsewhere in order to look at the works of the great masters, impressing everything securely in his memory. He knows amazingly well how to paint his inventions on to copper plates and although he is not very productive, he does it excellently well. He is good-natured and obliging to everyone. In this year 1604, he is about 28 or 30 years old.

2. Giulio Mancini, *Considerazioni sulla Pittura* (c. 1614–21), eds. Adriana Marucchi and Luigi Salerno. Rome 1956.

> *Di Adamo.*
>
> *Venne a Roma di terra todesca Adamo intorno agl' anni di Christo 1600 e, praticando con pittori italiani, subito prese la lor maniera; dove ha operato in picciol con tanto disegno, fine, colorito e gratia che è meraviglia et in particulare quando fa le cose di notte.*
>
> *Di suo si vedono poche cose perchè ha operato poco e quel poco è in mano di prencipi o di persone che, acciò non gli sien levate di mano, le tengon ascose. Parte delle sue opere sono state tagliate dal cavaliere ★★★, suo amicissimo, col quale vi fu qualche disgusto; che rappacificatosi nella malatia, non lasciò questo cavaliere officio di cordialissimo amico.*
>
> *Morì a questi anni con gran dolor e disgusto di quelli della professione che lo conoscevano. Fu sepellito honoratamente dalla*

Nattione et accompagnato alla sepoltura da. Pittori.

Translation.

On Adam.

He came to Rome from Germany about the working with Italian painters, quickly adopte He worked on a small scale with such design and grace that it is marvellous, particularly in

One sees little of his work because he proc this little is in the hands of princes and those p order that they should not be taken from th hidden. Some of his works were engraved by ★★★, his great friend, with whom however h During his illness they became reconciled an behaved like the greatest of friends.

He died recently to the great sorrow and sh his profession who knew him. He was bur honours by his countrymen, and accompanie by the painters of the Academy.

3. Giovanni Baglione, *Le Vite de' Pittori, Scu ed Intagliatori dal Pontificato di Gregorio XIII. d tempi di Papa Urbano VIII. nel 1642.* Rome, 16

> *Vita di Adamo Tedesco, Pittore.*
>
> *Dicono, che la palma sotto il peso si solleva talvolta sotto la fatica manca; ne v'è robustezz contrasti, se dal riposo non ha ristoro.*
>
> *In questi tempi fu Adamo da Francfort Tede figurine picciole era eccelente Pittore, e le operav arte, e maestria; e con gran gusto, e buon c invenzione le conduceva, ov'era tanta grazia, i qualsivoglia pittore paragonar si poteva.*
>
> *Ed in quel genere picciolo accompagnava sì fatti del naturale accordavano assai con quelle f vivo dipinte; e facevano mirabile armonia.*
>
> *Vago di perfezionare i lavori vi consumav sicchè bene spesso terminava il lavoro, e'l guad. tutti d'insegnamento, che nelle opere il compac deve esser l'onore. Non si vedono in pubblico perchè operò poco, ed in forma, che nel pubblico a*
>
> *Fu gran danno il perdere tant' uomo così presto cose (benchè picciole) avrebbe a pro della virtù la*
>
> *Morì giovane di dolore di stomaco, dicono dipingere sì picciole cose con tanto studio, ch'egli cogliere il frutto della virtù, indebolissi nel fiore de alla vita vinto dalla fatica.*

Era di bello aspetto, ed aveva presenza di nobile. Ebbe per moglie una Scozzese, e per potere più agiatamente vivere, era dal palazzo Apostolico lor somministrata ragionevol provvisione.

Va in volta di suo una carta finta di notte con una Maga, e con atti d'incantesimi, che rappresentano gli orrori dell'ombre, e gli spaventi dell'arte, opera assai bella, come anche di lui altre carte si ritrovano.

Morì qui in questa mia patria nel Pontificato di Paolo V. Romano; e il suo ritratto nell'Accademia di S. Luca, per eternare la sua memoria, si vede.

Translation.

They say that the palm grows upwards even under a weight; but ability under strain sometimes fails, and strength cannot withstand force if it is not refreshed by rest.

During this period [i.e. the Pontificate of Paul V] there was Adam of Frankfurt, the German. This was the excellent painter of small figures which he had rendered with the greatest skill and mastery. These he created with great taste, good design and rare invention, and with such delicacy and vividness, so that he could be compared with any painter.

And on this small scale he also painted such beautiful landscapes which, being taken from nature, accorded with these figures—all vividly painted and producing a miraculous harmony.

Eager to perfect his works, he took a long time over them, thus often leaving incomplete his work and with it his profit: these are all the signs that in work the companion of ability must be honour. One does not see his works in public, because he painted little, and in such a size that in any public exhibition they would have remained unnoticed.

It was a great loss to lose such a man so early, since he would have left some excellent works (though small ones) as evidence of his ability.

He died young of a stomach complaint, it is said, caused by painting so many small pieces with so much effort; in his efforts to bring his talents to fruition, he declined in the prime of his life, and died of exhaustion.

He was a good-looking man and of noble presence. He was married to a Scotch lady, and in order to be able to live in comfort, the Apostolic Palace administered to them a reasonable subsistence.

I once saw a print depicting a night-piece with a Sorceress and with all kinds of spells which represented the horrors of the underworld, and the terrors of the magic arts—a work so beautiful as other works of his have been found to be.

He died in my native town, during the Pontificate of Paul V; and his portrait can be seen in the Accademia di S. Luca, to perpetuate his memory.

4. Joachim von Sandrart, *Academie der Bau-, Bild- und Mahlerey-Künste.* Nuremberg 1675 (ed. A. R. Peltzer, Munich 1925).

Einer der aller berühmtesten und höchstgepriesenen Meistere in der edlen Mahlkunst war Adam Elzheimer, insgemein Adam von Frankfurt genant, eines Schneiders Sohn, neben der rothen Badstuben zu Frankfurt im Jahr 1574 gebohren. Der bey ihm verspührten grossen Begierde zur Mahlkunst zu Folge begab er sich auf das Zeichnen und folgends zu Philipp Uffenbach in die Lehr, und weil sein edler Verstand nur nach der grösten

Vollkommenheit gezielet, durchreisete er bald Teutschland, um fürters nach Rom zu gelangen, wie er solches auch werkstellig gemacht und daselbst sich allezeit zu den Berühmtesten und Tugendsamesten gestellet, dern damalen unterschiedliche als Peter Lastmann, Jann Pinnas von Amsterdam, Jacob Ernst Thoman von Lindau und andere mehr sich allda befunden, die insgesamt den höchsten Gipfel der Vollkommenheit zu erreichen sich beflissen, und gleich wie unser Vatter Adam der erste gewesen unter allen Menschen, also ware dieser der erste Adam, der in der Mahlkunst kleinern Bildern, Landschaften und andern Curiositäten sich also hoch und natürlich erhoben, dass er ein Vorgeher und Vatter worden, dessen Manier als die aller-vollkommensten, auserlessnesten und natürlichsten in allen Theilen alle andere Mahler nachgefolget.

Unter andern seinen bästen Werken mehrte er seinen Ruf mit einem kleinen Tobias auf ein Kupferblättlein einer Spannen lang, worinn der Engel den jungen Tobias durch ein seicht-rinnendes Wasserbächlein zu kommen behülflich ist und das Hündlein von einem Stein zu dem andern springet, als begierig hinnach zu kommen, beyden scheinet die aufgehende helle Sonne ins Angesicht. Die Landschaft ist so schön, der im Wasser erscheinende Wiederglanz des Himmels so natürlich, die Reisende und Thiere dermassen wol gebildet, dass dergleichen wahre Manier vorhin niemals gesehen, und dahero in ganz Rom von nichts dann von Elzheimers neu-erfundener Kunst im Mahlen geredet worden. Gleicher Weisse mahlte er in eine etwas grössere Landschaft eine Latona mit beeden Kindern, dero die im Gemöss arbeitende Bauren das helle Wasser zum Trinken missgönneten, desswegen sie zu Fröschen verwandlet worden. Ferner in selbiger Grösse die verwundte und nackende Procris, der durch gesunde Kräuter ihr Cephalus zu helfen sich bemühet, von weiten sind die Feldgöttinnen, Satyren, Fauni, Alt und Junge, die ein Feuer vor dem Wald aufmachen, gebildet. Nicht weniger künstlich ist sein Gemähl, wie S. Lorenz vor dem Richter entkleidet wird, ihne folgends auf dem Rost zu braten bey dem allda gestellten Abgott, der sich aber andächtig zum Himmel wendet mit unbeschreiblichen affecten, welches original jezo bey dem hochgeboren Reichsgrafen und Herrn, Herrn Johann von Nassau, zu Saarbrucken in seiner Residenz neben vielen andern Raritäten zu sehen. So mahlte er auch noch einen kleinen heil. Laurentium für meinen Vettern Abraham Mertens von Frankfurt, der in einem gebildten Levitenrock in einer Hand den Rost, in der andern den Palmzweig hält, zuruck aber eine weit hinaus sehendes Gebürg, Thäler und Wasserfallen, mit zierlichem Bauwerk, wordurch die Abendsonne strahlet, dermassen ungemein natürlich und tiefsinnig, dass zum genugsamen Lob mir mehr die Reden als materi zu seinem Lob ermanglet. Nach so hoch-gepriessner neu-angenommener Manier in Oelfarbe der kleinen Stucken, hat er das gross mahlen (welches doch sein erstes studium war) verlassen und ist bey dem kleinen verblieben.

Er etzte auch etliche kleine Landschaften, wie die Feldgötter und Nymphen mit Cymbalen tanzen, auch die Satyren aufspielen und andere dergleichen vernünftige Selzsamkeiten. Mehr bildete er eine Tagröthe von einem finstern Wald, da man über weit entlegene Gebürg und Thäler biss zu dem Horizont hinsihet, alles sehr verwunderlich coloriert, wiederum in kleiner oval-Form die Enthauptung des heiligen Johannis des Täuffers, worinnen er eine grosse Vernunft in Erkantnus der einigen wahren Manier, die Nachtstucke zu mahlen, genugsam an Tag gegeben, welches dann so hoch gepriesen worden, dass er hierdurch angefrischet ferners gebildet hat, wie Jupiter und Mercurius von weiter Reise ermüdet in dem schlechten Bauren-häusslein der Pausae und Philemonis eingekehret und bey einem Lampenlicht nidergesessen, wovon sie selbst neben diesen armen Leuten und ihrem Hausrähtlein also vernünftig beleuchtet werden, dass dieses und folgendes Werk eine ganze Instruction und Lehrschule, wornach man die gerechte Nachten ergreiffen und lernen mag, und bekenne ich, dass ich in meiner Jugend selbst, wie ich Nachten zu mahlen angefangen, dieses für eine Ideam, Richtschnur und formular gehalten. Eben so künstlich ist das grosse Werk der trinkenden Ceres bey Nacht, die bey einem alten Weib mit der Kerzen stehet und von deren schalkhaften Buben verspottet wird, so alles theils wegen der herrlichen Ordinanz und Invention, theils wegen der Zeichnung, Colorit, unterschiedlicher schönen Lichtern, Landschaften, Bäumen, empor stehendem und herabhangendem Laubwerk, Blättern und Kräuteren billig das höchste Lob, Ruhm und Preiss erhält.

Wie hoch dieser schöne Geist in der Poësie, Allusionen, Inventionen und guten Gedanken gestiegen, beweist sein allergrötes Werk in seiner Geburtstadt, welches mir der hochbenahmte Handelsherr Du Fay Anno 1666 gezeiget, worinnen das Contento oder die Vergnugung auf ein grosses Kupferblatt folgender Gestalt ausgebildet. In der Luft schwebet das Verlangen oder Contento in zweyen anmuthigen Bildern vorgestellet, unten her auf der Erden sind allerley hoch und niedere Standspersonen in ihrem Vornemen beschäftiget, etliche zeigen ihre Hoffnung zu den Göttern mit Andacht bey dem Opferfeuer, da in einem finsteren Tempel der weiss-bekleidte alte Priester mit dem Rauchwerk in Gegenwart der mit Lorbeerzweigen gekrönten Vestalischen Jungfrauen, als auch der antichen Ordnung nach junger Knaben mit Weyrauchskästlein samt andern Zubereitungen des Altars, auf dem das Opferfeuer brennet, wovon die herum stehende Andächtige wunderlich beleuchtet werden. Vornenhero sihet man das zur Schlachtung geführte Opfervieh. Im Tempel oben herunter komt der erschröckliche Jupiter mit seinen blinkenden Donnerkeylen in der Hand, als der sich wegen des angezündeten Opfers ganz willfährig gegen dem Contento erzeiget. Ausserhalb des Tempels zeigen sich allerley Standspersonen sehr geschäftig, jeder nach der Art seines Verlangens, begirig zu hoher Dignität, Pracht, Gut und Geld, die Philosophi und andere zur Gelehrtigkeit, Kunst und Weisheit, etliche durch Handlung und Kriegs-Verrichtungen ihren Gewinn zu erlangen, andere durch schnell lauffen, mit Pferd rennen, mit spielen, keglen und andere Mittel, ihren Contento zu erlangen, deren jedwedere auf absonderliche Weis und ganz ungemeine Manier vorgestellet, dass selbiges Stuck für dieser Stadt gröste Zierde in der Mahlkunst zu preisen.

In einem andern grossen Stuck hat er die Flucht in Egypten mit dem Kindlein Jesus, das unser liebe Frau in ihren Mantel eingefasst und auf einem Esel sitzt, ausgebildet; den durch ein mit Kräutern erfülletes Wässerlein gehenden Esel führet Joseph, welcher in der andern Hand einen brennenden Span zum Nachtlicht träget. Von weitem sihet man die Feldhirten mit ihrem Vieh bey einem brennenden ins Wasser scheinenden und reflectirenden Feuer, vor ihnen einen dicken Wald, über welchen an dem heitern Himmel das Gestirn, sonderlich die Jacobsstrasse, hinten her aber noch verwunderlicher der klare volle Mond, als bey dem hintern Horizont neben den Wolcken aufgehend und seinen Widerschein in das Wasser ganz vollkommen werfend,

abgebildet zu sehen, desgleichen vorhero nie
worden und ein Werk, das in allen Theilen z
einem jeden besonderlich ganz unvergleichlich is
seine Werk, deren er wenig, jedoch fürtreffli
Kupfer, so wol von Magdalena de Pas als ander
das Originalstuck aber hat mir Junker Gauda v
besonderer Liebhaber der Kunst, sehr oft gezeigt
er sich oft unterstanden, dasselbe auf das alle
Kupfer nach zu stechen, hat er doch niemalen dess
Fürtreflichkeit erreichen mögen, wie dann unm
Kupferstecher-Kunst dem Mahlen völlig gleiche
ob schon dieses Gauda Kupferstuch andere
beschämen doch die Original-Gemälde obgedacht
wann wir eines derselben dagegen setzen, ja es we
davon verfinsteret, gleichwie das irdische Licht
Sonnen verfinsteret und beschämet wird.

Also tiefsinnig verfärtigte Elzheimer seine We
Gedächtnus und Verstand war dergestalt abgeri
er nur einige schöne Bäume angesehen (vor welc
ja ganze Täge gesessen oder gelegen), er selbi
eingebildet, dass er sie ohne Zeichnung zu Ha
natürlich und ähnlich können nachmalen, wi
daran zu sehen, dass nach dem er zu Rom die V
sich also imprimirt, er selbige ohne einige
höchster Curiosität in seine Landschaften auf
gebracht, jeden Baum absonderlich nach seiner
Laub und Blättern in allen Theilen erkantlic
Schatten und reflexion ganz ähnlich, naturäl und
Weis zwar nicht eines jeden Thuns, auch sehr s
Beyhülf des Lebens oder Nachzeichnung die S
bringen. Endlich machte ihn diese schwäre Weis
melancholisch, darzu er ohne das geneigt gewe
Hauswirthschaft schlecht vorgestanden, unang
Römerin geheuratet und mit ihr viel Kinder bek
er auch dürftig gewesen, ob ihme schon seine
bezahlet worden. Also wurde er überdrüssig, stec
in Schulden, und muste obgemeldter Gauda
schossenen Gelds auf seine unausgemachte Arb
lang zu Rom mit schwären Unkosten warte
Elzheimer darüber Schulden halber in die Ge
worden, worinnen er sich doch selbsten wiede
billig thun können und sollen) durch Arbeit ge
sich darüber sehr betrübet, also dass er gar erkra
zwar erlediget worden, hat er doch bald hernac
unsterblichem Lob und Nachklang aller Fürtreffl
gesegnet. Dessen Wittib, von der ich ein Werk
zu Rom mit etlichen nachgelassenen Söhnen no
von welchen weiters Lob zu erwehnen ich geliebte
dieser Orten abstehen und noch dieses zum Schl
dass er pflegte nicht allein jederzeit schwäre
nehmen, sondern auch solche auf das glücklic
führen. Alle seine Verrichtungen übertraffen
Künstler Gedanken sehr weit. Er war in der V
und im guten so fest gegründet, dass wann er mi
Kreiden nur einen Umriss gemachet, er dar
Verstand zeigte, als andere durch unverdrosse
Arbeit konten zu Wege bringen. Seine W
nimmermehr in flüchtiger Bewegung, noch in a
Zier oder Kralenfarben, sondern vornämlich
Stücken in der auserlesensten Zeichenkunst

Colorirung, also dass, wann man seine Gemähle durch einen Spiegel gegen das natürliche Leben angesehen, eines wie das andere sich ereignet, als ob es eine Sache gewesen wäre. Und dieses Lob hatte er in der weiten und breiten Welt, dannenhero auch alle fürnehme Liebhabere wie auch fremde curiose Reisende mit höchstem Verlangen von dieser berühmten Hand etwas rares und sonderbares in seiner Geburtsstadt Rahthaus zu sehen vermeinen, weil er insgemein der Adam von Frankfurt genennet wird, und ob man zwar gänzlich hätte dafür halten sollen, es werde selbiger löblicher Magistrat in dessen Rahthaus unter andern sonderbaren Raritäten gleichfalls von dieses Preis-würdigen Subjects vortreflichen Werken sehr viel besitzen, wie dann billig seyn solte und sonst allenthalben so der Gebrauch, massen Rom mit des Raphaël d'Urbino, Florenz mit des Michaël Angelo, Venedig mit des Titians, Basel mit des Holbeins, Nürnberg mit des Albrecht Dürers, Leyden mit des Lucas Leydens und andere Städte mit andern der ihrigen Kunststücken in ihren Rahthäusern nicht wenig prangen und denen Fremdlingen und Durchreisenden als auserlesene Kost-barkeiten zeigen und zeigen lassen, so ist doch in besagtem Frankfurter Rahthaus von ihme nicht das geringste zu sehen, noch seines Namens gedacht, ohnangesehn man daselbst darzu genugsame Mittel und Gelegenheit so wol vorzeiten gehabt, als noch heut zu Tage hätte. Dessen allen aber unerachtet, so wird gleichwol dieses Preiss-würdigen Künstlers Ruhm und Lob nicht erleschen, sondern es wird mit ihm heissen:

So lang man wird Tugend lieben,
So lang man wird Künste üben,
So lang wird man sich befleissen
Den Elzheimer hoch zu preisen.

Translation.

One of the most famous and highly praised masters in the noble art of painting was Adam Elsheimer, generally called Adam of Frankfurt, the son of a tailor, born in Frankfurt next to the 'Rothe Badstuben' in the year 1574. Because he felt a great urge to paint he began to draw and subsequently went to study with Philipp Uffenbach. Because he aimed at greatest perfection he soon travelled through Germany in order to get to Rome. This he managed to do and there he joined the most virtuous and famous. Among those who found themselves there, in order to gain the highest peak of perfection, were such different painters as Pieter Lastman, Jan Pynas of Amsterdam and Jacob Ernst Thoman of Lindau, and others. Just as our forefather Adam was the first man, so this Adam was the first to paint small pictures of landscapes and other curiosities in which he reached such heights that he became a predecessor and father whose manner has been imitated in all regions by all other painters as being the most perfect, the most select and the most natural.

Among his best works which increased his reputation was a small Tobias painted on a little copper-plate the width of a hand in which the angel helps the young Tobias to traverse a shallow brook, whilst a little dog jumps from one stone to the next eager to catch up with them. Both are illuminated by the bright rising sun. The landscape is so beautiful, the reflection of the sky in the water so natural, the travellers and animals so well rendered, that nothing like it has ever been seen before and hence the whole of Rome talked about nothing but of Elsheimer's newly discovered art of painting.

In the same manner he painted a slightly larger landscape with Latona and the two children, to whom the peasants, working in the bog, begrudge the clear water for drinking, because of which they are being changed into frogs. Further-more, he painted in the same size the wounded and naked Procris, whom Cephalus tries to save through healing herbs. In the distance are field-goddesses, satyrs, fauns, old and young, who kindle a fire in front of the wood. No less skilful is his painting of St. Lawrence, who, being disrobed before the judge before being roasted on the gridiron in front of the pagan god, turns his gaze to heaven. This is an indescribably moving work, of which the original can now be seen in the residence of Count Johann von Nassau at Saarbrücken amongst many other rarities. He also painted another small St. Lawrence for my cousin Abraham Mertens of Frankfurt, in which the figure is seen clad in a highly wrought chasuble, in one hand the gridiron, in the other the palm branch, in the background a wide vista with mountains, valleys, waterfalls, tiny buildings all illuminated by the evening sun. The whole is so naturally and imaginatively rendered that I lack words rather than matter to praise it adequately. After this much admired, newly acquired way to paint in oil on a small scale, he abandoned painting on a large scale (which was his first manner) and continued painting small.

He also etched several small landscapes in which field-gods and nymphs dance with cymbals, and satyrs make music and other equally clever curiosities. Furthermore, he painted an Aurora against a dark wood with a view over distant mountains and valleys to the horizon—all marvellously coloured. Again in small oval form the decapitation of St. John the Baptist in which he showed his great skill in the only true method of painting night pieces. This was subsequently so highly praised that, stimulated by it, he painted also the story of how Jupiter and Mercury arrived, tired from a long journey, in the poor peasant hut of Baucis and Philemon. They had sat down and were illuminated, like the two poor people and their utensils, from the light of lamps, in such a manner that this and the following work became a school and lesson from which one could learn how to paint darkness properly, and I admit that I myself in my youth took these works for my guideline and pattern when I started to paint night pieces. Equally skilful is the great work of Ceres drinking by night whilst she is standing by an old woman with a candle and is being mocked by an impudent boy. This work deserves the highest praise partly because of its marvellous design and invention, partly because of the drawing, the colour and the different beautiful lights, the landscape and trees as well as the hanging foliage, leaves and ferns.

What heights were reached by this genius in poetry, invention and imagination is shown by his greatest work, which was shown to me in his native town by the famous merchant DuFay in the year 1666, in which is depicted the Contento or Indulgence on a large copper panel in the following manner. In the air hovers Desire or Content depicted in two charming figures; below on earth several personages of high or low rank busy themselves, some worship the gods with devotion round a sacrificial fire, whilst in a dark temple the old priest, dressed in white, stands with the incense in the presence of Vestal Virgins crowned with laurel leaves, accompanied by youths in antique dress carrying vessels with caskets of incense and other implements for the altar, on which burns the sacrificial fire, by which the surrounding congregation are miraculously illuminated. In the front one sees the animals about to be slaughtered. From above the temple descends the terrible Jupiter with glittering thunderbolts in his hand, angrily noticing the sacrificial fire which has been lit for Contento. Outside the temple several personages are busy each according to his desires, eager for high position, splendour, wealth and possessions; the philosophers and others for scholarship, art and wisdom; others for gain through action and preparation for war; others again through sports such as running, horse-racing, bowling and gaming—all to gain content. All this has been rendered in such an original and curious manner that it must be for this town one of the greatest ornaments of the art of painting.

In another big piece he depicted the Flight into Egypt in which the Madonna sits on an ass and covers the child Jesus with her cloak. Joseph, lighting the way with a burning torch in one hand, leads with the other the ass through a little brook bordered by plants. In the distance one sees herdsmen with their animals near a burning fire, which are reflected in the water. In the background a thick forest, above which are depicted in the clear sky the stars and especially the Milky Way and even more miraculously the clear full moon, which rises above the clouds on the horizon, and whose reflection is perfectly rendered in the water, in a way which has never before been attempted. This work is incomparable both in the whole of its parts and in each individual part, as were all his works, of which he painted few, but excellently well on copper and which were used by Magdalena de Pas and others for engraving. The original, however, was often shown to me by Cavalier Goudt in Utrecht, a particular admirer of his art. And although he often attempted to engrave it on copper as faithfully as possible he was never able to reach complete excellence, because it is impossible that the art of engraving can equal that of painting. Although Goudt's engravings excel others, these engravings show up their inferiority when they are compared with the original paintings from which they were made—they are diminished in the same way as the earthly light is diminished and shamed by the clear sun.

So profound were Elsheimer's works, for his memory and imagination were thus constituted, that if he only saw a few beautiful trees (before which he had often sat or lain half or even whole days) they were so firmly engraved on his mind that he was able to render a complete and natural likeness of them at home, without preliminary drawing. This can be judged by the fact that he impressed the Vigna Madama in Rome so firmly in his mind that he was able to incorporate it without any drawings and with greatest skill into his landscapes. Every tree is recognizable from its special type, from its stem, foliage and leaves in all parts as well as from colour, shade and reflection, quite similar, natural and vivid, a manner which not everybody can achieve and which is difficult without the aid of the actual object or a drawing. However, this difficult way of working made him finally tired and melancholic, as was his temperament in any case, and he neglected his domestic duties, for he married a Roman lady and had many children by her, hence he was poor although he received high payments for his

works. Thus he became weary, ran into de
above mentioned Goudt had to encounter gr
Rome because he had advanced him money f
was not being completed. As a result Elsheim
the Debtor's prison, where he did not even l
working (as he could and should well have do
so melancholic that he even became ill and al
freed, he died soon afterwards in Rome,
praise and echoes of his excellence. His
whom I was able to acquire one of his work
Rome in 1632 with several surviving sons, w
of brevity prevents me from praising here any
want to mention finally that Elsheimer not c
attempted difficult things, but he was also able
them splendidly. All his renderings surpass
intentions of many other artists. His techniqu
grounded that even when he only drew an ou
or chalk, he showed more understanding tha
able even after steady painstaking effort. His
consisted in fleeting movement, nor in m
embellishment or loud colours, but above all
way in perfect draughtsmanship and natural
that if one compares his paintings with rea
mirror-image, one would resemble the other.
reputation in the wide, broad world, that all
noisseurs, as well as eager foreign travellers,
something rare and important from his famou
townhall of his native city, because he is uni
Adam of Frankfurt. And whilst Rome boasts
of Urbino, Florence with Michelangelo, Venic
Basle with Holbein, Nuremberg with Alb
Leiden with Lucas van Leiden, and other citi
native works of art in their townhalls to sho
and tourists as choice rarities, the noble
Frankfurt, which has a townhall filled with c
works of art, cannot show a single work by th
his name commemorated, although there wa
and there is even now, the means and the op
acquire some. In spite of this, however, the fa
of this praiseworthy artist will not fade, but it
of him:

> As long as virtue will be loved
> As long as the arts will flourish
> So long one will be eager
> To praise Elsheimer highly.

5. Jean-Baptiste Le Brun, *Galerie des Peintres . . .*

ELZHEIMER, (ADAM)
Élève de Philippe Offenbach.

*Adam Elzheimer naquit à Francfort en 1574. Sor
aperçu de son inclination pour la peinture, le plaça c
Offenbach, bon peintre. Elzheimer quitta l'Al
voir l'Italie. Ce fut là qu'il se fit cette manière de
finir en petit, qui lui a si bien réussi. Il fut le m
siècle dans ce genre.*

*Les tableaux de ce maître sont autant de chefs
finesse de son pinceau est d'autant plus étonnant
l'a pas empêché d'avoir une couleur riche et une touc
Ses ouvrages sont très-rares aujourd'hui: on en tro*

tout qui soient bien conservés; et c'est alors qu'ils sont vendus très-cher; mais il faut se défier d'un grand nombre de copies faites par Thoman, Téniers le père, Bamboche et le comte de Goud. Beaucoup d'autres peintres ont aussi copié Elzheimer avec succès; et lorsque ces tableaux sont du tems de ce dernier, il faut une véritable connaissance et un examen réfléchi pour ne pas les confondre avec les originaux.

Le petit Moyse, connu sous le nom de Uytenbroeck, a gravé plusieurs sujets de la fable, des paysages et des animaux de sa composition, dans le genre d'Elzheimer et de Corneille Poelembourg.

Le comte de Goud, appelé Henri Goud, a gravé sept tableaux d'Elzheimer avec beaucoup de finesse et d'effet. Ce peintre a gravé lui-même quelques pièces de sa composition.

Il mourut à Rome en 1620.

Le prix des ouvrages de ce Maître s'élève jusqu'à 6000 liv. et plus, selon leur richesse et leur composition. Celui que nous avons fait graver a été vendu 1000 liv. Ses plus capitaux, quoique généralement rares, se rencontrent en Allemagne. Comme il glaçait beaucoup en peignant, on les trouve souvent fatigués par l'ignorance de nettoyeurs.

Disciples d'Adam Elzheimer
JACQUES ERNEST THOMAN

HAGELSTEIN *l'a copié et imité de manière à tromper du vivant même de son maître.*

Il a encore été copié par COSSIAU, *peintre de l'électeur de Mayence, de la maison de Schoenborn. Celui-ci a peint plusieurs tableaux dans la ménagerie de Versailles. Il naquit près de Breda, et mourut septuagénaire à Mayence en 1732 ou 33.*

Translation.

ELSHEIMER (ADAM)
Pupil of Philipp Uffenbach

Adam Elsheimer was born at Frankfurt in 1574. His father, realizing his son's inclination for painting, placed him with Philipp Uffenbach, a good painter. Elsheimer left Germany to see Italy. It was there that he learned this manner of paint-ing and finishing in a small format of which he made such a success. He was the best in the field in his time.

The paintings of this master are so many masterpieces; the delicacy of his brush is all the more astonishing for not preventing the achievement of rich colouring and a soft touch. His works are very rare today, and even so, one finds few which are well preserved, and therefore these fetch high prices; but one has to be on one's guard about a great number of copies made by Thoman, Teniers the Elder, Bamboche [i.e. Pieter van Laer who left for Italy in 1623 and arrived in 1625] and Count Goudt. Many other painters also copied Elsheimer with success, and when these paintings are from his time, it needs real connoisseurship and careful examination not to confuse them with the originals.

The little Moses, known under the name of Uytenbroeck, engraved several subjects of fables, landscapes and animals, being his own compositions in the manner of Elsheimer and Cornelis Poelenburgh.

Count Goudt, called Hendrick Goudt, has engraved seven paintings by Elsheimer, with great skill and effect. This painter has himself engraved several pieces of his own composition.

He died in Rome in 1620.

The price of the works of this master goes as high as 6000 livres and more, according to their richness and their composition. The one we had ourselves engraved [i.e. by Joseph Maillet] was sold for 1000 livres. His most excellent ones, although generally rare, are found in Germany. As he often used glazes a lot in painting, one finds them often over-cleaned through the ignorance of restorers.

Pupils of Elsheimer
JAKOB ERNST THOMAN VON HAGELSTEIN

Hagelstein copied him and imitated his manner to the point of deception in his master's lifetime. He was also copied by [Jan Joost van] Cossiau, painter to the Elector of Mainz at the castle of Schoenborn. This painter also painted several works in the 'ménagerie' at Versailles. He was born near Breda, and died in his seventies in Mainz in 1732 or 33.

1 *Design for an Armorial Window* (Cat. 28). 1596. Pen and wash, 313 × 203 mm.
Düsseldorf, Kunstmuseum

2 *Fama* (Cat. 27). About 1596. Pen and wash,
150 × 91 mm. Karlsruhe, Staatliche Kunsthalle

3 *The Witch* (Cat. 1). About 1
Oil on copper, 135 × 98 m
Hampton Court Palace, Royal C

4 *Adam and Eve* (Cat. 52). About 1597. Engraving, 203 × 163 mm. Brussels, Bibliothèque Royale

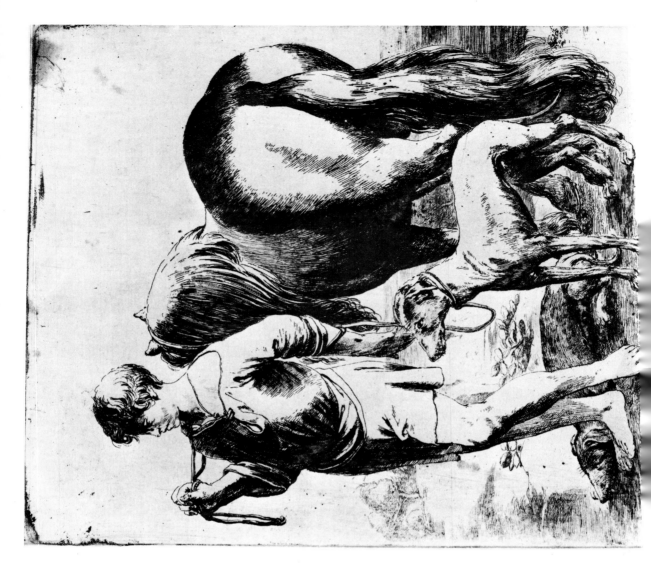

5 *Allegory of Fortune* (Cat. 53). About 1597.
Etching, 118 × 95 mm.

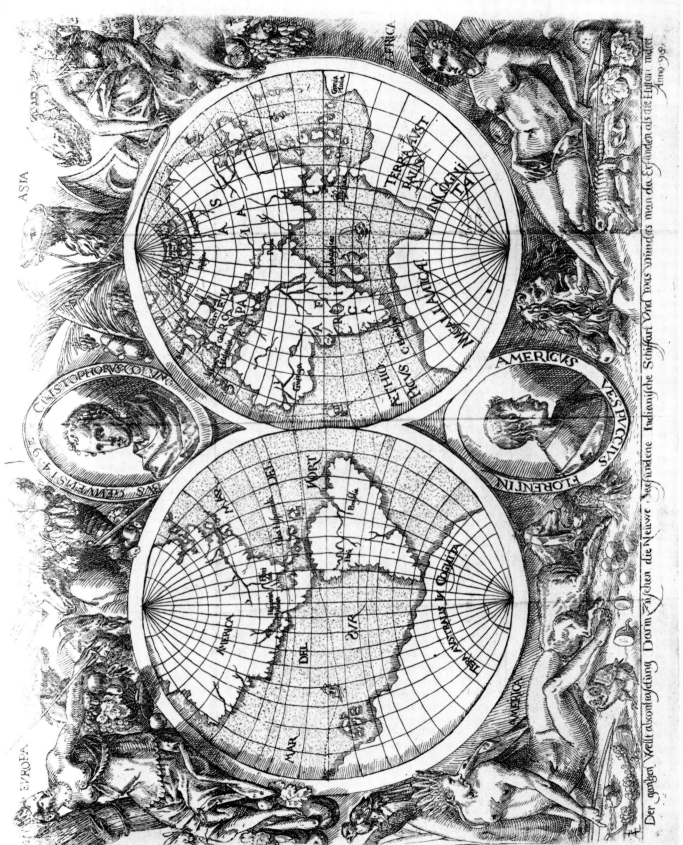

7 *Map of the Two Hemispheres with Portraits of Columbus and Vespucci* (Cat. 55). 1598. Etching, 229 × 300 mm.

8 *The King of Bali and his Retinue* (Cat. 29). 1598. Pen and grey wash, 109 × 144 1
Copenhagen, Statens Museum for Kunst

9 Unknown artist: *The King of Bali and his Bodyguards.* 1597. Engraving

10 *South African and Malay Native Types* (Cat. 55). 1598. Etching, 229 × 300 mm.

11 *Native Types from Sunda, Sumatra and Java* (Cat. 55). 1598. Etching, 229 × 300 mm.

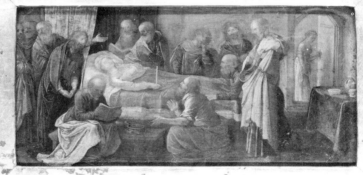

12 *House-Altar with Six Scenes from the Life of the Virgin* (Cat. 2). About 1597–8. Oil on copper, *c.* 360
Berlin–Dahlem, Staatliche Museen

13 *The Coronation of the Virgin.* 260 × 210 mm. Detail from Plate 12

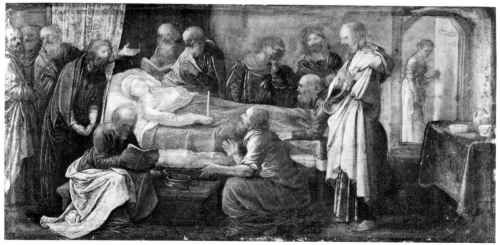

14 *The Death of the Virgin.* 100 × 210 mm. Detail from Plate 12

15 *The Annunciation*. 120 × 100 mm. Detail from Plate 12

16 *The Visitation*. 120 × 100 mm. Detail from Plate 12

17 *The Nativity.* 120 × 100 mm. Detail from Plate 12

18 *The Adoration of the Kings.* 120 × 100 mm.
Detail from Plate 12

20 *The Conversion of Saul* (Cat. 4). About 1598–9. Oil on copper, 195 × 250 mm. Frankfurt, Städelsches Kunstinstitut

21 *St. Christopher* (see Cat. 5, copies).
Oil on copper, 230 × 164 mm.
Windsor Castle, Royal Collection

22 *St. Christopher* (see Cat. 5, c
Oil on copper, 239 × 183 n
Windsor Castle, Royal Colle

23 *St. Christopher* (Cat. 5). About 1598–9. Oil on copper, 225 × 175 mm. Leningrad, Hermitage Museum

26 *The Denial of Peter* (Cat. 33). Pen and brown ink, 125 × 168 mm. Zürich, Kurt Meissner collection

24 *A Painter Presented to Mercury* (Cat. 30). 1598. Pen and wash, 87 × 143 mm. Braunschweig, Herzog–Anton–Ulrich Museum

27 *The Flood* (Cat. 6). About 1599. Oil on copper, 265 × 348 mm. Frankfurt, Städelsches Kunstinstitut

28 *The Baptism of Christ* (Cat. 8). About 1599. Oil on copper, 281 × 210 mm. London, Nation.

29 *The Holy Family with the Infant St. John* (Cat. 7). About 1599. Oil on copper, 375 × 243 mm.
Berlin–Dahlem, Staatliche Museen

31 *The Burning of Troy* (Cat. 11). About 1600–1. Oil on copper, 360 × 500 mm. Munich, Alte Pinakothek

32 *Large Sheet of Figure Studies* (Cat. 34). 1600–1. Pen and brown ink, 265 × 192 mm.
Berlin–Dahlem, Staatliche Museen

33 *St. Lawrence Being Prepared for Martyrdom* (Cat. 9). About 1600–1. Oil on copper, 267 × 206 mm. London, National Gallery

34 *A Judgement Scene* (Cat. 31). Pen and ink, 184 × 120 mm.
Amsterdam, Rijksmuseum

35 *Jupiter and Mercury*
(Cat. 46). Pen and brown
Berlin–Dahlem, Staatli

36 Judith and Holofernes (Cat. 12). About 1601–3. Oil on silvered copper, 242 × 187 mm.
London, Wellington Museum, Apsley House

37 *Small Sheet of Sketches of Figures and Heads* (Cat. 35).
1602–3. Pen and brown ink, 178 × 111 mm.
Berlin–Dahlem. Staatliche Museen

38 *Studies of Figures, including Satyrs and a Carità Group* (Cat. 40). 1602–3.
Pen and wash, 97 × 180 mm. London, British Museum

39 *A Seated Bearded Man, in the Background Horsemen and Fleeing Figures* (Cat. 37).
Pen and brown ink, 86 × 140 mm. Berlin–Dahlem, Staatliche Museen

40 *Mountainous Landscape* (Cat. 42). 1602–3. Pen and brown ink, 176 × 265 mm.
Berlin–Dahlem, Staatliche Museen

41 *Pietà* (Cat. 36). About 1601–2.
Pen and brown ink, 69 × 55 mm.
Weimar, Kunstsammlungen

42 *Pietà* (Cat. 14). About 1603. Oil on copper, 210 × 160 mm. Swiss private collection

43 *The* Three **Marys** *at the Grave* (Cat. 13). About 1603. Oil on copper, 258 × 200 mm. Bonn, Landesmuseum

44 *Group of Angels on Clouds* (Cat. 39). Pen and wash, 109 × 201 mm. Berlin–Dahlem, Staatlich▪

45 *Angels Ministering to Christ* (Cat. 38). About 1603–5. Pen and brown wash, 87 × 197 r▪
Frankfurt, Städelsches Kunstinstitut

46 *The Stoning of St. Stephen* (Cat. 15). About 1603–4. Oil on silvered copper, 347 × 286 mm.
Edinburgh, National Gallery of Scotland

47 *The Finding and Exaltation of the True Cross* (Cat. 16). Reconstruction with fram

48 *The Exaltation of the Cross* (Cat. 16). About 1603–5. Oil on silvered copper, 485 × 350 mm.
Frankfurt, Städelsches Kunstinstitut

49 *The Empress Helena Embarking to Find the True Cross* (Cat. 16). About 1603–5.
Oil on silvered copper, 226 × 150 mm. Frankfurt, Städelsches Kunstinstitut (on loa

50 *Heraclius Carrying the Cross* (Cat. 16). About 1603–5. Oil on silvered copper, 226 × 150 mm. Frankfurt, Städelsches Kunstinstitut

51 *The Digging for the Cross* (Cat. 41).Pen, brush and wash, 156 × 155 mm. Hamburg, Dr Wilhelm Holthusen collection

52 *Heraclius.* Detail from Plate 54

53 *The Digging for the Cross* (Cat. 16). About 1603–5. Oil on silvered copper, 152 × 150 mm. Frankfurt, Städelsches Kunstinstitut (on loan)

54 *Heraclius on Horseback with the Cross* (Cat. 16). About 1603–5. Oil on silvered copper, 152 × 150 mm. Frankfurt, Städelsches Kunstinstitut (on loan)

55–60 *St. John the Baptist – St. John the Evangelist – St. Peter – St. Paul – St. Thomas
Aquinas – Tobias and the Angel* (Cat. 17 A–F). About 1605. Oil on silvered copper,
each 90 × 70 mm. Petworth House (National Trust)

61–62 *St. Anne and the Virgin – St. Joseph and the Christ Child* (Cat. 17 G–H).
About 1605. Oil on silvered copper, each 90 × 70 mm. Petworth House
(National Trust)

63 *St. Lawrence* (Cat 17 I). About 1605.
Oil on silvered copper, 90 × 70 mm.
Montpellier, Musée Fabre

64 Cornelis Poelenburgh after
Elsheimer: *Abraham and Isaac* (cf. Cat. 17).
Oil on copper, 100 × 70 mm.
Florence, Palazzo Pitti

65 *Joseph and the Christ Child* (Cat. 57).
Etching, 110 × 87 mm.

AURORA amsto noctem reclamine Sellens,
Ostatum vices reddit ab ore diem.
Goudt Palat. Comes, et Aur. Mil. Eques.

67 Hendrick Goudt after Elsheimer: *Aurora*. 1613. Engraving, 128 × 169 mm.

69 *Il Contento* (Cat. 44). About 1607. Pen and grey wash over black chalk, 288 × 374 mm. Edinburgh, National Gallery of Scotland

71 *Il Contento* (Cat. 19). About 1607. Oil on copper, 301 × 420 mm. Edinburgh, National Gallery of Scotland

72 *Tobias and the Angel* ('*The small Tobias*') (Cat. 20). About 1607–8. Oil on copper, Frankfurt, Historisches Museum

73 *Tobias and the Angel* (Cat. 47). Gouache, 70 × 95 mm. Berlin–Dahlem, Staatliche Museen

74 Hendrick Goudt after Elsheimer: *Tobias and the Angel*. 1608. Engraving, 133 × 189 mm.

75 *Tobias and the Angel* (Cat. 58). Etching, 92 × 146 mm.

76 *Apollo and Coronis* (Cat. 21). About 1607–8. Oil on copper, 174 × 216 mm. Corsham Court, Lord Methuen

77 *The Realm of Venus* (Cat. 22). About 1607–8. Oil on copper, 87 × 14
Cambridge, Fitzwilliam Museum

78 *The Realm of Minerva* (Cat. 22). About 1607–8. Oil on copper, 87 × 1
Cambridge, Fitzwilliam Museum

79 Hollar after Elsheimer: *The Realm of Juno* (Cat. 22). 1646. Etching, 90 × 170 mm.

80 Hollar after Elsheimer: *The Realm of Venus*. 1646. Etching, 94 × 148 mm.

81 Hollar after Elsheimer: *The Realm of Minerva*. 1646. Etching, 94 × 147 mm.

82 *The Mocking of Ceres*. Copy (Cat. 23). About 1608. Oil on copper, 295 × 241 m

83 *The Mocking of Ceres* (Cat. 50).
Gouache, 159 × 104 mm. Hamburg, Kunsthalle

84 *Ceres Changing the Mocking Boy into a Lizard*
(Cat. 51). Gouache, 110 × 68 mm. Zürich,
Kurt Meissner collection

85 *The Mocking of Ceres* (Cat. 56). About 1609. Etching, 284 × 227 mm. Hambu

86 Hendrick Goudt after Elsheimer: *The Mocking of Ceres*. 1610. Engraving, 291 × 236 mm.

88 Hendrick Goudt after Elsheimer: *Jupiter and Mercury in the House of Philemon and Baucis*. 1612. Engraving, 164 × 220 mm.

90 Hendrick Goudt after Elsheimer: *Tobias and the Angel*. 1613. Engraving, 197 × 256 mm.

Effugit in tenebris Lux mundi, et conditor orbis   *Rebus in adversis exemplum fine æmula Classis*

Exul apud Pharios latitat, res mea Tyrannes   *Quem semper teneti Fortuna exercuit usu*

H. Goudt Palat. Comes, et Auc. M. fec. et pes. 1613

92 Hendrick Goudt after Elsheimer: *The Flight into Egypt.* 1613. Engraving, 293 × 397 mm.

93 *Salome Receiving the Head of St. John* (Cat. 48). Gouache, 78 × 67 mm. Chatsworth, Trustees of the Chatsworth Settlement

94 Hendrick Goudt after Elsheim *Salome Receiving the Head of St. J* Engraving, 65 × 51 mm.

96 *Nymph Dancing with Tambourine and* Etching, 63 × 100 mn

95 *The Bath of Bathsheba* (Cat. 49). Gouache, 91 × 84 mm. Vienna, Albertina

97 *Self-Portrait* (Cat. 26A). About 1606–7. Oil on canvas, 637 × 480 mm. Florence, Uffizi

98 Hendrick Hondius: *Portrait of Elsheimer*.
Engraving, published about 1610.

99 Unknown artist: Copy of Elsheimer's
Self-Portrait. Oil on canvas, 610 × 470 mm.
Rome, Accademia di San Luca

100 Hollar: Portrait of Elshe
Etching, published 166

COMPARATIVE ILLUSTRATIONS

101 B. à Bolswert after Coninxloo: *Forest Landscape wi*
Engraving. Amsterdam, Rijksr

102 Uffenbach: *Calvary*. 1588.
Frankfurt, Städelsches Kunstinstitut

103 Uffenba   awing.
Göt

104 Dürer: *The Witch*. 1507. Engraving

105 Dürer: *The Resurrection*. 1510. Woodcut

106 Jobst Harrich: Copy after Dürer, *The Coronation of the Virgin* (from the Heller Altar). About 1614. Frankfurt, Historisches Museum

107 Altdorfer: Figure from *Susannah and the Elders*. 1526. Munich, Alte Pinakothek

108 Rottenhammer: *Ecce Homo*. 1597. Kassel, Staat

109 Rottenhammer and Brill (attrib.): *The Adoration o*
Hampton Court Palace, Royal Col

110 Jacopo Bassano: *The Flood* (copy). About 1580. Munich, Alte Pinakothek

111 Jost Amman: *Arrival of Turkish Ambassadors in Frankfurt*. Detail. 1562. Woodcut.
Oxford, Ashmolean Museum

SIC SALSAS FRVGES, SIC VINCTI TEMPORA VICTTIS THVRA DABANT,

H. Cock excudebat.

SIC VETERES QVONDAM, RECTIGENS INSCIA, DIVVM NVMINA PLACABANT, CÆSIS

112 Cornelis Cort: *Sacrificial Procession.* About

113 Adriaen van Stalbemt (attrib.): *The Preaching of St. John.* Ab···········othek

114 Rottenhammer: *Allegory of Art.* 1587.
Düsseldorf, Kunstmuseum

115 Venetian bronze: *Caritas.*
London, Victoria and Albert Museum

116 Hollar: *Mercury and Herse* (Cat. A19). Etching

117 Gabriel Weyer: *Athena as Patron of the Arts*. 1616. Berlin–D

118 Rubens: Copy of figures from Elsheimer's *Stoning of St. Stephen* (Plate 46).
Drawing, about 1606. London, British Museum

119 Copy of Elsheimer's *Il Contento* (Plate 71). Dated 1615. M.

120 N. Knüpfer after Elsheimer: *Il Contento*. About 1650. Muni

121 N. Knüpfer: *Il Contento*. 1651. Schwerin, Staatliches Museum

122 Rubens: Partial copy of Elsheimer's *Il Contento* (Plate 71). About 1620–30.
London, Count Antoine Seilern

123 Flemish mid–seventeenth century after Elsheimer (attrib.): *Tob...*
London, National Gallery

124 Copy after Elsheimer: *The Flight into Egypt* (cf. Plate ...

125 A. F. Oeser: *The Artist in his Studio* (with a copy of Elsheimer's
Salome receiving the Head of St. John, Plate 93, let into the easel).
Detail. 1732. Weimar, Kunstsammlungen

126 After Elsheimer: *The Realm of Venus*. (cf. Plate 77). About 1608.
Vienna, Akademie

127 C. Moeyaert: *The Meeting of Jacob and Esau*. Ab

128 Pieter Lastman: *The Sacrifice at Lystra*. 1614. Formerly

129 Jan Pynas: *The Raising of Lazarus*. About 1605–8.
Philadelphia, John G. Johnson Collection

130 David Teniers the Elder (attrib.): *Tobias and the Angel*. About 1604–5.
Paris, Fondation Custodia, F. Lugt Collection

131 Cornelis Galle I after Rubens: *Judith and*
Engraving

132 Claude Lorrain: Detail from *Pastoral L*
From the Collection at Parham Park

133 Rubens: *The Flight into Egypt.* 1614. Kassel, Staatliche Kunstammlungen

134 Hendrick Goudt(?): *Jupiter and Mercury with Philemon and Baucis.*
Wanås, Wachtmeister Collection

135 Rembrandt: *The Supper at Emmaus*. About
Paris, Musée Jacquemart-André

136 Rembrandt: *The Rest on the Flight into Egypt*. 1647. Dubli

CATALOGUE

Dimensions are given in millimetres.

PAINTINGS

1. The Witch. About 1596–7 (Plate 3)
Hampton Court, Collection of H.M. The Queen (Inv. 733).
Oil on copper, 135×98.

PROVENANCE: Sir Arthur Hopton (c. 1588–1650); Charles I.

LITERATURE: Abraham van der Doort, 'Catalogue of the
Collections of Charles I', ed. Oliver Millar, *Walpole Society*,
vol. XXXVII, 1960, p. 77; C. H. Collins Baker, *Catalogue of
Pictures at Hampton Court*, 1929, p. 41; W II, p. 90, No. 96
(as on wood); Waddingham 1972, p. 602, fig. 20; Andrews,
Münchner Jahrbuch, 1973, p. 162, fig. 5.

This little copper, a copy of Dürer's engraving (Pl. 104)—is
first mentioned in the 1639 inventory of the collection of
King Charles I, as having been given to the King by Sir
Arthur Hopton, who was Ambassador in Spain and may well
have acquired the painting during his continental travel (1629
or 1635). It is described in van der Doort's entry: 'Item a
little peece wherein painted a witch rideing upon a black
ram Goate in the Aire with a distaffe in her hand 4. little
Cupidds in—severall Actions by, said to bee done by
Elsehamer before hee went to Italie by a Printe of—
Alberdure, painted upon the righte lighte/5½ × 4.' Although
known in the literature since the middle of the seventeenth
century, the painting was first reproduced in Waddingham's
1972 article. At first sight the attribution to Elsheimer may
look strange and unconvincing, but on closer scrutiny it is
supported by certain characteristics, such as the transparent
modelling of the figures and the draperies, the claw-like hand
of the witch and the physiognomical resemblance of the
putto on the left to those who hover above the *Holy Family*
in the Berlin painting (Cat. 7). The wisps of grass in the
foreground and the transformation of the whole scene from
daylight into night may also be thought a typical Elsheimer
trait. It is interesting that the entry in van der Doort's
catalogue mentions particularly that the work was thought
to have been painted before Elsheimer left for Italy, as this
reinforces the conception of his apprenticeship in the German
tradition and his particular affinity with Dürer's work.

Weizsäcker mentions another version in the collection
Franz Jäger, Vienna (listed by T. Frimmel in *Berichte und
Mitteilungen des Altertumsvereines zu Wien*, XXX, 1890, p. 24),
which Waddingham has traced to a sale at Hirschler's,
Vienna, 26 April 1900, No. 14, with illustration.

**2. House-Altar with Six Scenes from the Life of the
Virgin.** About 1597–8 (Plates 12–18)
Berlin-Dahlem, Staatliche Museen, Gemäldegalerie (Inv. 664).
Oil on copper. Damages in central panel.
Side Panels: Left: *The Annunciation* and *The Nativity*; Right:
The Visitation and *The Adoration of the Kings*. 120×100.
Lower Panel: *The Death of the Virgin*. 100×210.
Central Panel: *The Coronation of the Virgin*. 260×210.

PROVENANCE: Berlin, Royal Collection; first catalogued in
1830; Kaiser-Friedrich Museum.

LITERATURE: *Verzeichnis der Gemäldesammlung des Königlichen
Museums zu Berlin*, 1830 (G. F. Waagen) (No. 174, as
'Netherlandish School, under Italian influence'); *Verzeichnis
... etc. 1860 (do.); Verzeichnis ... etc., 1878* (von Meyer &
Bode), as 'Manner of Elsheimer'; *Verzeichnis ... etc., 1883*
(as Elsheimer, youthful work); Bode, *Studien*, pp. 250 and
280; Weizsäcker, 'Elsheimers Lehr- und Wanderzeit...', in
Jahrbuch der Preussischen Kunstsammlungen, XXXI, 1910, p. 78
(with question mark); *Verzeichnis ... etc., 1912* (with
question mark: of a later period); Bode, in *Amtliche Berichte
aus den Königlichen Kunstsammlungen*, XXXVIII, No. 10, July
1917, cols. 246–7 (attribution to Elsheimer rejected); Drost,
1933, p. 64; Bothe, p. 42; W II, p. 69, pls. 17 and 18 (as
Hendrick v.d. Borcht); Andrews, *Münchner Jahrbuch*, 1973,
pp. 164 ff., fig. 11.

It is fascinating to follow Bode's vacillations between whole-
hearted acceptance, luke-warm indecision and total rejection
of this work as an original by Elsheimer. In 1883, in his
Studien and in the entry of the Berlin catalogue, which no
doubt was authorized by him, Bode arrived at the truth,
namely that the six panels are by Elsheimer himself and date
from his early years in Germany. The layout of the whole
altarpiece and in particular the composition of the central
part, *The Coronation of the Virgin*, depend strongly on Dürer's
Heller Altarpiece (Pl. 106), then still in the Dominican church
at Frankfurt. Bode further suggested (1883, p. 251) that the
tower in the background of *The Visitation* was based on the
old Eschersheimer Tor at Frankfurt, whilst Weizsäcker saw
in it less specific but more generalized echoes of Frankfurt
fortifications. Drost rightly recognized the resemblance of
some of the figures to those of the Petworth/Montpellier
panels (Cat. 17), obviously maturer and later works, painted

in Rome. From this he drew the wrong conclusion that the Berlin altarpiece must also date from Elsheimer's Italian years. But the difference in technical accomplishment is so great that the two works cannot date from the same period. It might be said that the Berlin altarpiece looks forward to the Petworth figures, and that when this series was done, Elsheimer recollected the roots of early German art, from which he sprang and which also provided the impulse for the *Scenes from the Life of the Virgin*.

As the Berlin altarpiece is so closely modelled on Dürer's *Heller Altarpiece*, it might be asked whether the latter also contained a predella painting.

3. Jacob's Dream. About 1597–8 (Plate 19)
Basle, Collection Robert von Hirsch.
Oil on copper, 196×262. Inscribed on the back with the mark C.8.

PROVENANCE: Duke of Norfolk; Sale, Christie, London, 11 February 1938, Lot 84; bought Matthiesen (together with *Conversion of Saul*, see Cat. 4).

LITERATURE: Waddingham 1972, p. 600, fig. 12; Andrews, *Münchner Jahrbuch*, 1973, pp. 171 f., fig. 13.

Although rubbed and somewhat damaged by overcleaning, and probably left unfinished in parts, there can be no doubt that the painting is by Elsheimer, dating from his German years. The figure of the sleeping Jacob stems from Dürer (woodcut of the *Resurrection*, Pl. 105—the sleeping soldier on the right) and was, incidentally, also repeated by Uffenbach in his print of the *Resurrection* (Andresen, 2). The background of dense woodland does, for once, look somewhat like that favoured by the painters of the Frankenthal school, and may have been influenced by them. The glory at the top of the heavenly ladder is incomplete, as is the similar passage in the *Conversion of Saul* (Cat. 4), possibly owing to rubbing or, more likely, to incompleteness. The painting, together with the *Conversion of Saul*, was in the collection of the Dukes of Norfolk, and may have been inherited from the Earl of Arundel, who owned several Elsheimer paintings (see p. 10).

4. The Conversion of Saul. About 1598–9 (Plate 20)
Frankfurt, Städelsches Kunstinstitut (Inv. 2107).
Oil on copper, 195×250. Much rubbed in parts and left unfinished.

PROVENANCE: Duke of Norfolk; Sale, Christie, 11 February 1938, Lot 84 (together with *Jacob's Dream*, see Cat. 3), bought Matthiesen; Private Collection, San Francisco.

LITERATURE: W. Heil, 'A newly discovered work by Adam Elsheimer', in *Miscellanea Leo van Puyvelde*, Brussels, 1949, pp. 221 ff.; M. Waddingham, review of Frankfurt exhibition 1966/67, in *Burlington Magazine*, January 1967, p. 47 (as F. van Valkenburgh); K. Bauch, review of Frankfurt exhibition 1966/67, in *Kunstchronik*, April 1967, p. 92 (as Antonio Carracci); VG I, pp. 141–2; M. Stuffmann, 'Miszellen zu zwei Bildern von Hans Rottenhammer und Adam Elsheimer', in *Städel Jahrbuch*, N.F., II, 1969, pp. 169 f.; Waddingham 1972, p. 601 (as Elsheimer); Andrews, *Münchner Jahrbuch*, 1973, pp. 169 f., fig. 12.

The highly dramatic, almost theatrical composition—unusual for Elsheimer—has given rise in the past to doubts as to

whether this is in fact an
Although the paint surface
picture seem to have been lef
doubt that it is by Elsheime
paint has worn thin, it is p
acteristic grey underpainting
horse on the right, and in p
for example). Stylistically th
altarpiece (Cat. 2) and *Jacob*
appears also to date from El

The recumbent figure o
soldier in the earlier battle-
stained-glass window—whic
He thus did not require the
(Tintoretto's *Miracle of St.*
by those who dated the
Venice. The various posture
to German sources: woodc
and Jost Amman. Heinric
attention to a possible
Bavarian paintings, such
paintings by Christoph
Bocksberger, with their o
Geissler, 'Eine Zeichnun
Schwarz', in *Münchner Jal*
turn owe a debt to Jost A
one, it might be suggeste
painted after Elsheimer ha
in the Munich region, en
VERSION: Sale, Christie,
Edinburgh), Lot 78: A. I
on copper; and *A Confla*

5. St. Christopher. Ab
Leningrad, Hermitage N
Oil on copper, 225×17

PROVENANCE: First rec

LITERATURE: Bode, *Stua*
30, No. 33; Andrews, *N*

No agreement has bee
extant versions of thi
Elsheimer's hand. The
recently cleaned, appea
grad, though largely c
be of better quality a
status, or another eve
Leningrad picture oug

The hermit, shinin
representations of the
(Dürer), the pose of th
hair, from Jost Amn
Reusneri, 1581, No. x
53), probably also th
W I, Pl. 3). But the
remote background
touches and recur in
Flight into Egypt). I
draperies in Dürer's
Elsheimer's are mor

bridge from Elsheimer's training in the German tradition to the first impact from the great Venetian masters (for example Tintoretto's *Agony in the Garden*, S. Stefano, Venice). In fact the head of the Saint reappears in the lower right corner of *The Flood* (Cat. 6), Elsheimer's first Venetian painting.

There seems to be a connection between the Elsheimer painting and the various versions made by Orazio Borgianni (Edinburgh, National Gallery of Scotland) to be dated about 1615. But Rubens too seems to have known the composition (or a version of it), for he copied, fairly freely, the Child and the Saint's head in a drawing in the British Museum (Inv. Gg.2.231), reproduced in Burchard-d'Hulst, *Rubens Drawings*, 1963, No. 43; J. S. Held, *Rubens: Selected Drawings*, 1959, No. 30, pl. 26. The painting may therefore have actually been, or been known, in Rome during the first decade of the seventeenth century, as the Rubens drawing seems to be a straight copy and need not have been made in Antwerp, after Rubens's return from Italy, as Held maintains.

VERSIONS: In the *Catálogo de la Galería de cuadros del Excmo. Sr. José de Madrazo* (Director of the Prado), Madrid 1856, No. 487, there is listed a *St. Christopher* by Elsheimer, on copper (23 × 18 cm) from the collection of the Marquesa de Canillejas. The painting has not been traced.

COPIES: (a) Windsor Castle (Inv. 2963). Copper, 230 × 164. Pl. 21. *Prov.*: Earl of Arundel; given to Charles I; v.d. Doort Cat., ed. O. Millar (op. cit.) p. 90, No. 75; 'The Inventories and Valuations of the King's Goods 1649–1651', ed. Oliver Millar, *Walpole Society*, XLIII, 1972, p. 257, No. 32: sold to Gaspars, 22 March 1649/50 for £33; Duke of Portland, 1757; Duke of Argyle; George Walker, Edinburgh; Francis 14th Lord Gray: *Catalogue of the Collection of Pictures . . . of Kinfauns Castle*, Perth 1828, p. 3, No. VI; still there in 1924, cf. *The Scottish Print Club: Catalogue of some objects of interest in Kinfauns Castle (Perthshire) on the occasion of a visit by the Club on 24 May 1924* (p. 11); by descent to Morton Gray Stuart, 17th Earl of Moray; Sale, Sotheby, 9 June 1932, Lot 34; bought by Queen Mary.
Lit.: Reveil, *Musée de Peinture et de Sculpture*, Paris (London) 1831, XII; G. Walker, *Descriptive Catalogue of a Choice Assemblage of Original Pictures*, 1807, I, p. 1, No. 1; W I, p. 102; W II, p. 30, No. 53.
Engraved by James Heath in 1812 when in the George Walker Collection (repr. W I, p. 33, No. 36).
Exh.: *The King's Pictures*, London, Royal Academy, 1946–7, No. 349; *Between Renaissance and Baroque*, Manchester (City Art Gallery), 1965, No. 85.
On the whole of inferior quality, and with damages (Saint's blue vest). Very superficial rendering of features and draperies, as well as of foliage. No build-up of tones. No bell above hermit. No reflection in water of torch and foliage.
(b) Windsor Castle (Inv. 96). Copper, 239 × 183. Pl. 22. *Prov.*: not known when it entered Royal Collection; probably at Kew in reign of George III. (Information from Sir Oliver Millar.)
Of better quality than Windsor 2963. Very thin paint, possibly overcleaned at some time. Almost like Bramer.
(c) Lady Victoria Wemyss, Wemyss Castle. Canvas on panel, 285 × 182. *Prov.*: Duke of Portland.
Very rough copy, probably by David Teniers II.

6. **The Flood.** About 1599 (Plate 27)
Frankfurt, Städelsches Kunstinstitut (Inv. 1607).
Oil on copper, 265 × 348. Marked with monogram AE on the bale in front. Inscribed on the back: 'Adam' and 'Adam Elshamer'.

PROVENANCE: South German Private Collection; acquired 1920.

LITERATURE: W I, pp. 63 ff.; Drost 1933, p. 36; W II, p. 5, No. 1.

EXHIBITION: Frankfurt 1966/67, No. 1.

The grey underpainting is visible in the lower margin and on the naked woman in the upper left corner, and there are pentimenti on the head of the woman bending over the bale.

This painting has always been assumed to have been one of the first, if not the first, designed in Venice. The head in the lower right corner reveals the same features as the St. Christopher (Cat. 5), which would suggest that the two paintings are close in date. The larger figures in the foreground echo Rottenhammer's to such an extent that one wonders if the older artist had perhaps a hand in designing them. The Venetian influence in the composition is strong. Indeed some of the details and especially the figures in the foreground and those floating in the water could have been derived from a painting of the same subject by Jacopo Bassano in Kromeriz (clearer studio copy in Munich, Inv. 6048; Pl. 110). This in turn seems to depend on a Florentine engraving of c. 1470–90 (Hind, III, pl. 197) which Baldung Grien must also have known, judging by his painting of 1516 at Bamberg. The animals swimming in the water probably derive once again from Jost Amman (for example the stag in the water), see *Venatus et Aucupium iconibus*, 1582, fol. K2. Michelangelo's *Flood* (Sistine Ceiling), which has on occasion been cited as an influence on Elsheimer, is unlikely to have been known to him before he came to Rome.

COPY: Late seventeenth century, Munich (Private Collection).

ENGRAVING: (left half, with some variations) by Philip Andrea Kilian, *Index Picturarum Chalcographicarum Historiam Veteris et Novi Testamenti . . . etc.*, Augsburg, 1758, fol. 5.

7. **The Holy Family with the Infant St. John.** About 1599 (Plate 29)
Berlin–Dahlem, Staatliche Museen, Gemäldegalerie (Inv. 2039).
Oil on copper, 375 × 243.

PROVENANCE: Stroefer, Nuremberg; acquired by the Museum in 1928.

LITERATURE: H. Voss, 'Elsheimers "Heilige Familie mit Engeln", eine Neuerwerbung der Gemäldegalerie', in *Berliner Museen*, 50, 1929, pp. 20 ff.; W I, pp. 67 ff., pl. 22; Drost 1933, p. 40; Möhle 1940, pp. 11 f.; W II, p. 18, no. 14.

EXHIBITIONS: *Aufgang der Neuzeit*, Nuremberg 1952, No. R2; *Deutsche Maler und Zeichner des 17. Jahrhunderts*, Berlin 1966, No. 7; Frankfurt 1966/67, No. 11, fig. 10.

The picture has often erroneously been called 'Rest on the Flight to Egypt', but the infant St. John disproves this description. The painting is, in spirit, close to Altdorfer's *Holy Family at the Fountain* of 1510 (Berlin), which has also been called a 'Rest on the Flight to Egypt'. It has often been remarked how similar in type and pose are the figures of Joseph in both pictures. Also the wreath of putti is reminiscent of Altdorfer, as is the treatment of light. Hence it is possible that Elsheimer saw the painting on his way to Venice in 1598.

However, the physiognomies, especially the face of the Madonna, are still very close to those of the larger figures in the *Flood*, and also show the influence of Rottenhammer. The foliage is more elaborate and evocative than in the *Flood* and the richly decorated cloth of the seated Angel's cloak is the first of many such highly wrought draperies, with which Elsheimer loved to attire some of his major figures.

8. **The Baptism of Christ.** About 1599 (Plate 28 and Col. Plate III)
London, National Gallery (Inv. 3904).
Oil on copper, 281×210.

PROVENANCE: Possibly J. Schuckborough decd. and others Sale, Christie, London 1 March 1771, Lot 59, The Baptising our Saviour, Elshamer—unsold at £3; Sale, Christie, London 27 March 1779, No. 70 (second day); bought Shriber; Sir Joshua Reynolds; Sale, Christie, London 14 March 1795, Lot 27 (fourth day); bought Dermer; probably Booth Sale, Christie, London 25 April 1812, Lot 132; bought Bowden; George Smith Sale, Christie, London 27 May 1882, Lot 16; bought Wagner; Henry Wagner; presented to the National Gallery, 1924.

LITERATURE: Bode 1920, p. 44; W I, pp. 66 f.; Drost 1933, pp. 38 ff.; W II, p. 20, No. 18; Michael Levey, *National Gallery Catalogues: The German School*, 1959, p. 43.

EXHIBITION: *Early German Art*, London, Burlington Fine Arts Club, 1906, No. 67.

The panel has recently been cleaned and it is now clear that the composition is not a 'conflation of three incidents into one scene', the Baptism—Christ summoning St. Peter from his boat—Peter removing the coin from the fish. As Weizsäcker had already suggested, the seated man in the foreground is merely removing his shoe, and the tiny scene at the left shows people arriving in a boat.

The strong Venetian elements (Tintoretto and Veronese) have always been stressed by previous writers, though the figures still owe a great deal to Rottenhammer's example. Yet there are also echoes from Altdorfer: the ring of putti is reminiscent of the *Birth of the Virgin* (Munich), then in the Cathedral at Regensburg.

This is the first painting with what has become accepted as a typical Elsheimer landscape background: wooded hills interspersed with occasional figures and towering buildings. It is also the first instance in which Elsheimer introduces a group of attendant figures in the middle ground, characteristic of many later compositions. Some of the figures are on horseback, often with turbans or plumed caps (see for example *The Stoning of St. Stephen*, Cat. 15).

COPY: Drawing in the École des Beaux-Arts, Paris (Inv. M.1129, as 'Poussin'). 302×264. Pen and brown ink, heightened with white, with traces of black chalk—to which Konrad Oberhuber drew my attention.

It is a seventeenth-century drawing, possibly German,

freely but faithfully copied,
very top has been transferre
the draughtsman ignored t
fitted the composition into

9. **St. Lawrence being pr**
1600–1 (Plate 33)
London, National Gallery (
Oil on copper, 267×206.

PROVENANCE: [The followi
are conjectural, as it canno
and the same painting is inv
is seamless.]

As Frans Francken made a
burg) and Pieter Soutman e
Antwerp in the second qu
On the other hand Sandrar
of Count Johann von Nass
1635; Sale S. Feitama, Am
Sale Eversdijk, The Hague
Sale, London, 9 April 1772
to the National Gallery ir

LITERATURE: Bode, *Studi*
p. 58; W I, pp. 70 ff., pl.
National Gallery Catalog
pp. 38 f.

The scene here is not the
martyrdom on the gri
treasures of the Church
Lawrence's martyrdom;
gestures of some of the
about to be put to death
Possibly Elsheimer rem
Gesuiti, Venice (another
includes a pagan idol, a
Titian, 1969, pp. 54 f., w
often depicted as havin
The statue of Hercules
Hercules as almost all
have stated. The body
head quite inappropriat
not copied from any kn
depend on a young Bac
of Praxiteles (versions i
of the Satyr, in form
interesting to observe t
ground of Raphael's *S*
stance and pose as th
Breenbergh, in his pair
(Frankfurt, Inv. 621),
wonders whether Po
remembered it when
Erasmus of 1628/29 (
wreathed Hercules.

The inscription on
letters, has not been i
to be all in Latin an
suggested. All one ca
capital letters FA in t

HE, which must stand for Hercules, in the third. A possibility might be lines 255-7 from Ovid's *Metamorphoses*, IX:

cunctisque meum laetabile FActum
dis fore cONfido. Siquis tamen HErcule, siquis
forte deo doliturus erit . . .

and Prof. Martin Ostwald (Swarthmore) has suggested the possibility that someone made up the following:

FActus Di-
ONysus est
HErcules

As to the architecture in the background: the temple at the right is somewhat like the Temple of Vespasian, though the frieze is incorrect, and the building in the farther background conforms to some extent to the tombs along the Via Appia or Via Latina (Annina Regilla or the one known as S. Urbano alla Caffarella). Both buildings may in fact intend to suggest Rome in general, rather than any specific pieces of architecture.

The oriental figure with turban, both in the foreground and middle distance—already foreshadowed to some extent in *The Baptism* (Cat. 8)—makes here its first major appearance. The equestrian soldier reappears, with variation, in *The Stoning of St. Stephen*, and the two youths stoking the fire make their appearance again in *Apollo and Coronis* and *The Flight into Egypt*, with alterations. The palm-carrying angel is no longer Venetian, but more specifically Roman, and Levey has suggested that it is a derivation from Marcantonio's engraving of *The Martyrdom of St. Cecilia* (B.117), which copies a Raphael School fresco.

ENGRAVINGS: Pieter Soutman (*c.* 1580–1657)—in reverse to the painting, repr. W I, pl. 26. A copy after Soutman's print is the etching by B. H. Lengin (W I, p. 145, No. 50).

COPIES: A long list of copies, some quite remote from the original, are given in W II, p. 32, amplified by Levey (pp. 39–40); the majority of them I have not been able to see or trace. To this list can be added a canvas in the Galleria Pitti Florence, at present on loan to the townhall at Bibbiena (Arezzo), which Marco Chiarini told me about.

10. St. Paul on Malta. About 1600 (Plate 30)
London, National Gallery (Inv. 3535).
Oil on copper, 170 × 213. Engraved on the reverse: *Costó mil doblones en Amberes*, i.e. Antwerp.

PROVENANCE: Possibly the 'Shipwreck of St. Pablo, small, by the hand of Adam', given to and endorsed by Dudley Carleton, by James Baptista Cresentio, possibly *c.* 1614. Since the middle of the eighteenth century in the collection of the Methuen family, Corsham Court, Wiltshire; Sale, Christie, 13 May 1920, Lot 16; bought Walter Burns; presented to the National Gallery in 1920.

LITERATURE: References to the painting when in the Methuen collection, see M. Levey (see infra); W. N. Sainsbury, *Original Unpublished Papers illustrative of the life of . . . Rubens*, 1859, p. 355; W I, pp. 177 ff., pl. 87; W II, p. 28, No. 31; M. Levey, *National Gallery Catalogues: The German School*, 1959, p. 42.

EXHIBITIONS: London, British Institution, 1857, No. 67; *Early German Art*, London, Burlington Fine Arts Club, 1906, No. 65.

Levey has argued that, although Antwerp is given, in the inscription on the reverse, as the place where the painting was purchased, the fact that this inscription is in Spanish would suggest that Sir Paul Methuen (died 1757) obtained it in Spain, where he was British Ambassador.

Stylistically, the *St. Paul* is close to *The Burning of Troy* (Cat. 11). The night effects, the 'fire-works' and the storm-laden sky are still in the northern, Bruegel, tradition. The rendering of the figures has matured since *The Flood*. They act as a foil for the violet-grey of the sky, the greenish-brown of the coastline and the black-green of the water, and their draperies provide the only colour in the otherwise sombre atmosphere. The figures are disposed in a row, as on a stage, and the only striking movement is the typically Elsheimer female figure, striding into the centre of the picture.

VERSION: Leningrad, Hermitage (Inv. 692). Panel, 545 × 830. By David Teniers the Elder. *Lit.*: Drost 1933, p. 49 (doubtful); W II, No. 128, pl. 37 (Dutch); Waddingham 1970 (David Teniers I); Vlieghe & Duverger 1972 (David Teniers I).

11. The Burning of Troy. About 1600–1 (Plate 31)
Munich, Alte Pinakothek (Inv. 205).
Oil on copper, 360 × 500.

PROVENANCE: Possibly the painting mentioned in the Inventory (1628) of the Elector Maximilian I of Bavaria: fol. 84 *In jezgedachter grösse ein Täffelin, darauf die Zerstörung Troye in die nacht gemahlt ist. No. 65* (Kreisarchiv, München, HR, Fasc. 24, No. 67); Düsseldorf; Mannheim (1730), where in the Inventory of 1756, it is listed under No. 78: *Der Brand von Troja, Aeneas seinen Vater Anchises davon tragend, reich von Figuren. Von Adam Elsheimer. Höhe: 1 Schuh 1 Zoll—Breite: 1 Schuh 6 Zoll.*; since 1802 back in the Electoral collection in Munich; transferred to Alte Pinakothek 1836.

LITERATURE: E. Plietzsch, *Die Frankenthaler Maler*, 1910, p. 98 (rejects attribution to Elsheimer); Bode, *Studien*, pp. 270, 279; do., 1920, pp. 22 and 46 f.; W I, p. 174, pl. 87; Drost 1933, p. 41, pl. 11; W II, pp. 49 f., No. 52; *Catalogue Alte Pinakothek: Deutsche und Niederländische Malerei*, Munich 1963, pp. 30 f.

EXHIBITIONS: *Aufgang der Neuzeit*, Nuremberg 1952, No. R3; Frankfurt 1966/67, No. 29, fig. 27.

Whether the painting mentioned, without measurements and artist's name, in the 1628 Munich Inventory is in fact the one by Elsheimer is not clear—it could have been the copper by Jan Bruegel the Elder, also in the Alte Pinakothek (Inv. 832). As, however, the painting (as Elsheimer) appears in Düsseldorf and Mannheim, where some of the paintings were transferred after the War of Succession, to be returned eventually to Munich in 1802, it might be presumed that it was in the Elector's possession by 1628, together with *The Flight into Egypt* (Cat. 26) and *The Preaching of St. John* (Cat. A12), now attributed to Adriaen van Stalbemt.

The subject was a favourite one with Flemish artists, and apart from Jan Bruegel, painters like Schoubroeck, Gillis and Frederick van Valkenburgh and Keunink, all tackled it. In Italy, the best known painting, before Elsheimer's time, is Barocci's canvas of 1598. While Elsheimer's composition depends to a great extent on the Flemish prototypes mentioned above, his figures show a sculptural feeling which may reflect his awareness of the Venetian and Roman masters. The multifigured design, with its flickering lights, is a reflection of Netherlandish night pieces, as well as those by the Bassani. The rich colouring is still very Venetian, whilst the architectural background, though imaginary, shows the first vaguely classical buildings in Elsheimer's work. The figure of Creusa is close to the *Judith* (Cat. 12), so that both paintings were likely to have been made in close proximity.

COPIES: (a) Seventeenth-century copy. Brukenthal Museum, Sibiu, Romania (Inv. 348). Copper, 420×540.

(b) Leonaert Bramer, chalk drawing in album of copies after paintings by contemporary artists. Amsterdam, Rijksprentenkabinet Inv. A704 (13th sheet, marked No. 55). See E. W. Moes and C. Hofstede de Groot (*Oud Holland*, 1895, pp. 182 and 238). As all the other paintings copied by Bramer can be traced to works that were in Delft between *c.* 1642 and 1654, it is likely that his prototype was a copy after the Munich painting.

12. Judith and Holofernes. About 1601–3 (Plate 36) London, Wellington Museum, Apsley House (Inv. WM 1604–1948).

Oil on silvered copper, 242×187. Fleur de Lys blind-stamped in lower right corner. Mark on back: *H 67 L/S.*

PROVENANCE: P. P. Rubens (listed in Inventory of 1640); sold from his estate to King Philip IV of Spain; the Fleur de Lys occurs on some paintings which belonged to or were appropriated by Elizabeth (Isabella) Farnese, wife of Philip V; the painting was captured 1813 as booty by first Duke of Wellington.

LITERATURE: Mentioned in Catalogues of Apsley House from 1901 onwards; W I, p. 98, pl. 33; Möhle 1940, p. 14; W II, pp. 10 f., No. 6; K. Andrews, 'Judith and Holofernes by Adam Elsheimer', in *Apollo*, September 1973, p. 207.

EXHIBITIONS: *Between Renaissance and Baroque*, Manchester, 1965, No. 84; Frankfurt 1966/67, No. 3, pl. 3.

There is damage in the extreme right corner, under the table, and craquelure on face and chest of Judith as well as on the body of Holofernes. There is also a pentimento on the right arm of Holofernes.

The figure of *Judith* is very close in type to that of Creusa in *The Burning of Troy* (Cat. 11). It is, as far as is known, Elsheimer's first composition set in an interior and his first painting on a 'silvered' copper plate (see Appendix). It is also his first picture in which the illumination springs from two candles. This, as well as the lovingly depicted still-life on the table on the right, may be a reflection of the tradition of still-life painting in Frankfurt, which artists such as Daniel Soreau and Georg Flegel continued in Elsheimer's native city. Elsheimer may still have known Flegel and his work before he left for Italy.

The painting was certainly in Rubens's collection, but not in that of Cornelis van Geest, as Julius S. Held, among many other writers, maintained ('Artis Pictoriae Amator', in *Gazette des Beaux-Arts*, Vol. L, July–August 1957, p. 67, n. 30a). The painting depicted in Willem van der Haecht's painting of Cornelis van der Geest's collection (Antwerp, Rubenshuis) is not that by Elsheimer, nor is it the one listed

in van der Geest's inventory
now also in the Prado (J.
kamers' in de 16e en 17e eeu
now in the Prado under de
totally different compositio
Coster.

13. The Three Marys at t
Bonn, Landesmuseum (Inv
Oil on copper, 258×200.

PROVENANCE: Paul Bril (16
Ottavia Sbarra (1629) *Uno
nera di uno sepolchro di Ad*
Faustina Baiocco *Le tre M*
Salucci [sic], *maggiore di gre*
(1712) *Le Tre Marie al sep*
[the preceding informatic
published by D. Bodart,
Paul Bril', in *Mélanges d'*
au professeur Jacques Lava
Otto Wesendonck (Kata
No. 144, as Elsheimer) by
Wesendonk [sic]; on loar
Berlin 1904–9; Bonn, Rh
with the Wesendonck co

LITERATURE: Bode, 19
Gemäldegalerie Bonn, 19
pl. VII; E. Buchner, '
Elsheimer', in *Sitzungsb*
Wissenschaft, 1950, Heft
review of Frankfurt exh
p. 60; G. Krämer, 'D
Elsheimer', in *Städel Jah*

EXHIBITIONS: *Aufgang
No. R14; *Deutsche Ma*
Berlin 1966, No. 9; Fra

In spite of the error o
ventory, it seems almo
Paul Bril's possession :
traced, through vario
Cardinal Origo into t
(1580–after 1660), wh
not Adamo, was a wit
architectural decoratio
pointed out that a pain
inventory of the poss
death in 1629 (W II, p
name of artist or size o
it cannot be the sam
collection never left t
seventeenth century.

This has been one
deal of controversy h
Möhle attributed the
thought of a painter
and Bauch (*Münchner
it to Lastman himsel
an attribution to Elsl
Frankfurt exhibition

ascription to Hagelstein.) It was indeed a seminal work: for both Jan Pynas's *Raising of Lazarus* (Pl. 129) and Lastman's *Entombment* of 1612 (Lille) would be unthinkable without it. Unusual is the full inscription of a passage from St. Mark's gospel on the lid of the tomb.

Almost all students of the picture have seen in the upraised hands of the central figure a direct borrowing from Caravaggio's *Deposition* (Vatican), which must have been painted at much the same time (*c.* 1602–3). However, this gesture of lamentation is a familiar one—almost a formula—which, to name only two examples, occurs in engravings by Jean Mignon, *The Rape of Proserpine* (Herbet 39) and *Le Perfide Sinon introduit par les bergers dans le camp des Troyens* (Herbet 15), both based on drawings after Luca Penni (Courtauld Institute and Louvre).

Stylistically the painting is close to the *Judith* and the little *Pietà* and like them should be dated to the early Roman years.

14. Pietà. About 1603 (Plate 42)
Swiss Private Collection.
Oil on copper, 210×160.

PROVENANCE: Possibly the painting mentioned in the 1610 Inventory (fol. 861r): *Un quadretto In Rame della Pieta corniciato et indorato, alquanto vecchio*; Gallery Harding, Vienna (1954); Private collection, London; K. Meissner, Zürich (1956); Private collection.

LITERATURE: E. Schaffran, in *Weltkunst*, XXIV, 1954, No. 4, p. 7 (as Friedrich Sustris); K. Bauch, 'Aus Caravaggios Umkreis', in *Mitteilungen des Kunsthistorischen Institutes in Florenz*, VII, 1953–65, pp. 235 f.; Waddingham 1967, p. 47; Andrews, 1972, p. 598; Waddingham 1972, p. 605.

EXHIBITION: Frankfurt 1966/67, No. 17, fig. 16.

The inscription 'Rome 1560', which at one time disfigured this panel, has since disappeared, as a later addition, during cleaning. As suggested (Andrews, op. cit.), it is basically an original by Elsheimer, but has been left unfinished. It is quite clear, in front of the original (less so from a reproduction), what passages are autograph and which have been over-painted. The former comprise the foliage on the left and the little still-life with the carafe; the right hand of the Virgin and the left arm and hand of Christ; the two faces have not been completed and the draperies have only been sketched in. The putti are not from Elsheimer's hand and have been heavily and crudely overpainted.

According to Bauch, Robert Eigenberger saw the connection with Elsheimer, but thought it to be a 'school' work. Bauch and Waddingham accepted the painting as a whole as autograph, and Waddingham, following Bauch, saw in it the influence of Annibale Carracci—possibly the panel at Naples (Posner 119), though they gave no specific instance. Bauch, in later years, accepted the author's assessment that the painting must have been left unfinished by Elsheimer.

The moving intimacy of the figures reflects, more than any compositional resemblances to Carracci, something of the tenderness and resignation of Michelangelo's group in St. Peter's. The subject of the painting has been interpreted as the Virgin anointing Christ's body, but what is possibly depicted is the Virgin shrouding the body of her Son.

DRAWING: Weimar, see Cat. 36.

15. The Stoning of St. Stephen. About 1603–4 (Plate 46 and Col. Plate 1)
Edinburgh, National Gallery of Scotland (Inv. 2281).
Oil on silvered copper, 347×286.

PROVENANCE: Paul Bril (1626); by inheritance to his widow Ottavia Sbarra (1629) *Uno quadretto in rame di una lapidatione di Sto. Stefano di lunghezza palmi uno e uno quarto*; by descent to the daughter Faustina Baiocco (1659) *Una lapidatione di S. Stephano di mano di Adamo Salucci* [sic], *con il paese di Paolo Brilli, in rame di palmi uno e mezzo incirca*; Cardinal Curzio Origo (1712) [the preceding information is taken from the documents published by D. Bodart, 'Les Tableaux de la succession de Paul Bril', in *Mélanges d'archéologie et d'histoire de l'art offerts au professeur Jacques Lavalleye*, Louvain, 1970, pp. 11–14]; Herzog von Braunschweig, *c.* 1775–80; sold by him to a merchant in Hamburg (see J. D. Fiorillo, *Geschichn der zeichnenden Künste in Deutschland und den vereinigtete Niederlanden*, 1817, vol. II, p. 553: *Ich erinnere mich, dass vor ungefähr 40 Jahren der Herzog von Braunschweig für einen billigen Preis ein schönes Gemählde von Elzheimer kaufen konnte, welches die Martern des heil. Stephanus vorstellte; das aber nachher an einen Hamburgischen Kaufmann verkauft wurde*); The Very Rev. G. D. Boyle, Dean of Salisbury (1828–1901); by descent to the last owner, from whom it was purchased by the National Gallery of Scotland in 1965.

LITERATURE: I. Jost, 'A newly discovered painting by Adam Elsheimer', in *Burlington Magazine*, 1966, p. 3; I. Bergström, 'Oeuvres de Jeunesse de Rembrandt', in *L'Oeil*, No. 173, May 1969, p. 2, fig. 4; C. Thompson and H. Brigstocke, *National Gallery of Scotland: Shorter Catalogue*, 1970, p. 27.

EXHIBITIONS: *Deutsche Maler und Zeichner des 17. Jahrhunderts*, Berlin, 1966, No. 10; Frankfurt 1966/67, No. 21, fig. 19.

It is curious to note that it was thought, when the painting was in the possession of Paul Bril's descendants, that the landscape was the work of Bril himself. The landscape background, such as it is, is indeed rather Bril-like, but is totally consistent with that in *The Baptism* or *St. Lawrence*, and is undoubtedly from Elsheimer's hand; especially the tiny figures in the trees and those interspersed with some of the background can only be by Elsheimer and cannot be separated from the environment into which they have been set.

Rubens must have known the painting, for, as Jost was the first to point out, the drawing by him in the British Museum (Hind, II, p. 19, No. 44), is composed with one exception, from figures taken from the Elsheimer (Pl. 118). The drawing was engraved by Pieter Soutman and exists in three states, two with the caption 'Adam Elshamer Inven.', the third without Elsheimer's name and with the inscription 'P.P.Rub. pinxit'.

Stylistically, the *St. Stephen* is close to the other painting of martyrdom, the *St. Lawrence*, but the hesitation and some-what stiff composition, still evident in the latter, has here been overcome in a crowded but immensely confidently handled composition. Previous commentators have seen in the semi-nude youth behind the Saint an echo of a similar boy in Caravaggio's *Martyrdom of St. Matthew* (S. Luigi dei Francesi, Rome), which probably dates from the same period as Elsheimer's painting. Waddingham's suggestion that the figure of the stone-thrower behind the Saint reflects the impact of Saraceni seems not convincing to me. Colin Thompson believes that this figure is taken from Vasari's paintings of the same subject (S. Stefano, Pisa, and in the Vatican), a striding figure, but also posed at the edge of the composition. Jost suggests that the inspiration came from a sculptured figure of *Marsyas* now in the Uffizi, but in Rome during Elsheimer's time (see also the drawing from the circle of Mantegna, Sale Sotheby, 26 November 1970, Lot 33). It is interesting to note that exactly this figure has been omitted in a copy (see below), which, though differing in some details from the original, is of high quality. The seated figure in the lower left, on an antique relief-fragment, is the young Saul (later Paul), 'consenting unto his death' (Acts 8:1), whilst Möhle saw in the standing youth on the extreme right a self-portrait of the artist.

As van Gelder has shown (vG-J I, pp. 146 ff.), several of Elsheimer's closest associates have incorporated figures and motifs from the *St. Stephen*: David Teniers I in his rendering of the subject (only known through an engraving by E. van Panderen, vG-J I, fig. 4) and his *Adoration of the Kings* at Aachen (vG-J I, fig. 8); Rubens's sketch *The Adoration of the Kings*, 1609 (Groningen); Jacob Pynas's *Adoration of the Kings*, signed and dated 1617 (Wadsworth Atheneum, Hartford) repeats the equestrian figure in the background of Elsheimer's painting. These artists must have seen the original in Rome, yet its impact was carried by these northerners to their homeland—to which they returned respectively in 1605 and 1608—and it found repercussions in the work of the young Rembrandt (*St. Stephen*, 1625, at Lyon, and *Balaam and his Ass*, 1626, at Paris, Musée Cognacq-Jay)—probably conveyed through Lastman, who in his *Sacrifice of Isaac* (grisaille, Amsterdam, Rembrandthuis) incorporates an angel very close to the one that brings the martyr's palm in the Elsheimer. But the most curious and striking derivation of Elsheimer's painting can be seen in Moeyaert's etching *The Meeting of Jacob and Esau* (Pl. 127) from the series of *The Story of Jacob* (Hollstein 14) which condenses—in reverse of course—the main accents of Elsheimer's composition.

COPY: A painting on silvered copper (350×291) was sold at Christie's, 10 December 1976, Lot 79. It lacks the figure of the stone-thrower and the large angel, top left. Although of very good quality, especially in the landscape background, this copy must date from about 1630.

16. The Finding and Exaltation of the True Cross.
About 1603–5 (Plates 47–50, 52–54, and Col. Plate II)
Frankfurt, Städelsches Kunstinstitut (6 and 7); Städelscher Kunstverein, on loan to the Städel (1, 3 and 5).
Oil on silvered copper.

(1) Left: The Empress Helena embarking to find the True Cross. 226×150. (Inv. 2131.)
(2) Bottom left: The questioning of the Jew. (Still missing.)
(3) Bottom middle left: The digging for the Cross. 152×150. (Inv. 2118.)
(4) Bottom middle right: The laying of the Cross upon a sick man. (Still missing.)
(5) Bottom right: Heraclius on horseback with the Cross. 152×150. (Inv. 2119.)
(6) Right: Heraclius carrying the Cross. 226×150. (Inv. 2054.)

(7) Middle: The Exaltation
2024.)

PROVENANCE: Juan (Giova
Grand Duke Cosimo II of F
of Norfolk; Sale, Christie,
(7 and 6), as 'The Resurre
Cross'; bt. Colnaghi; acqui
respectively; sale Christie,
(3 and 5); (1) acquired from

LITERATURE: J. Martinez,
arte de la pintura, etc., ed. M
'Notes on Art in Italy, n
Elsheimer', in *Apollo*, VI,
Holzinger 1951, p. 212; W
'An unpublished document
Tabernacle', in *Burlingto*
Waddingham and Ch. W
the Frankfurt Tabernacle
p. 192; I. G. Kennedy, '
Frankfurt Tabernacle', in

EXHIBITION: Frankfurt 19

Orbaan was the first to dr
altarpiece through the do
Medici archives in Flor
correspondence between
Cosimo II of Tuscany in
the acquisition of the al
recommended. At first, c
painter Cigoli, who wa
sale of the work from
delayed. Seven years la
renewed, as the Spania
and was demanding a l
whom Guicciardini, the
was the Cardinal del N
pleted and the altarpiec
mas. A sketch of the c
showing the disposition
With Holzinger's recog
panels which came to t
stones of the mosaic we
by one, three other p
Isles, which leads one to
must have been disme
were in the collection
that the whole was in
Two of the little pred

Whether the *Glor*
Martinez in the passa
altar must remain dou
of Elsheimer, Pl. 98,
the easel), but the co
the work is striking.
1620s, by which tim
The 'great painter' l
reports that he was fr

'At a certain occas
among the entourag
shown a painting, re

figures, with so much expression, dignity and skilful contrasts, that it amazed both connoisseurs and laymen. The great painter, who had taken me with him for the inspection, was asked what he thought of it (for it was for this purpose that he had been called). He answered that the painting was so excellent and well thought out that he believed nothing could be better made. It was certain that if the figures were to be enlarged to natural size, it would outshine all previous paintings.

This painting is from the hand of a Flemish painter who had studied in Rome for fifteen years, called Adam del Samar. The figures of this painter do not exceed a "tercia". He was of a very hermit-like and meditative nature and walked along the streets so wrapped in contemplation that he did not speak to anyone who addressed him. He judged himself a lesser artist than he in fact was; his friends remonstrated with him to change his manner, by putting more trust in himself, which was his due. His answer always was, that when he himself was satisfied with his works he would heed their advice.'

Elsheimer concentrates in his narrative on the search and discovery of the Cross, as related in chapter 68 of Voragine's *Golden Legend*, and on the Exaltation of the Cross (chapter 137). However, he must also have consulted another source, for in the scene in which Heraclius returns triumphantly on horseback with the Cross to Jerusalem (5), the *Golden Legend* states that a single Angel appeared to him and bade him to dismount and carry the Cross, humbly and barefoot, into the Holy City. Almost invariably the Angel is shown in pictorial renderings of this scene, and not a Bishop, as in Elsheimer's narrative. But Daniele de Volterra in his frescoes of the story of the *True Cross* in SS. Trinità dei Monti (destroyed c. 1799–1809) included, according to Félibien, *Entretiens sur les . . . plus excellens Peintres*, 1666, IV, p. 241, the Patriarch Zacharias of Jerusalem *lui donnant avis de quitter les habits superbes dont il étoit revêtu, il se couvrit d'un simple vêtement, & déchaussa ses souliers, pour mieux imiter l'humilité de Notre Seigneur . . .*. The source may have been a passage in Flavio Biondo's *Historiarum ab inclinatione Romani imperii decades III*, written in the 1440s and first published in Venice in 1483 and frequently reprinted. The accounts of Zacharias, who was patriarch from 609 to 628/9, differ as to whether he was liberated from the Persians by Heraclius together with the Cross or whether he died in captivity. If Elsheimer accepted the latter version, it is possible that he depicted him as a vision and not as a living person.

The middle panel refers to the Feast of the Exaltation of the Cross (14 September) and shows the elevated Cross surrounded by Saints and figures from the Old and New Testaments. St. Helena kneels at the foot of the Cross, surrounded by Angels carrying the instruments of the Passion. On the right, as a group, are Moses, Abraham, David and Daniel, below him Jonah. Opposite are Saints Dominic, Francis and Nicholas, with the Magdalen and St. Catherine below, and in the foreground St. Sebastian and the Latin Fathers of the Church: Pope Gregory, Saints Jerome, Ambrose and Augustine. On the bottom right the Martyrs Stephen, Lawrence and above him St. George. In the upper regions one can see the twelve Apostles, some of the Elders of the Apocalypse and Adam and Eve. At the very top a procession of angels accompanies the Virgin being crowned by the Trinity.

The Adoration of the Cross, sometimes adored by holy personages, was known from engravings (for example, Beatrizet's print of 1557, or the engraving by Adriaen Collaert), but Elsheimer's combination of it with the Coronation of the Virgin is no doubt based on such prototypes as Tintoretto's *Paradise* (Louvre) and Rottenhammer's *All Saints* (Earl Spencer). And very probably he also saw in Rome (Gesù) Franceso Bassano's *Paradise*.

Compositionally the sequence of the six panels depicting the search for and final restitution of the Holy Cross is unusual. They are grouped in rectangular U-shape around the central panel, but both the first (Helena's embarkation) and the last (Heraclius carrying the Cross) show a clear direction towards the right, whereas one would have expected a leftish tendency in the case of the latter, so as to encapsule the composition of *The Exaltation of the Cross*. As this must, however, have been a deliberate device, it has to be assumed that Elsheimer resorted to it in order to separate clearly the earthly events from those of the supernatural vision, and not lead one into the other.

PRELIMINARY DRAWING for Panel 3: see Cat. 41.

COPIES: (a) *The Exaltation of the Cross*, anon. seventeenth century. Copper, 503×376. Coll. Bernard Houthakker, Amsterdam.

(b) do. (in reverse) by J. G. Kiss. Panel, 820×450. Signed and dated: 1642. Sale Vienna (? Kende), 25 April 1921.

(c) Two figures (Ambrose and Augustine) from central section. Possibly by Poelenburgh. Red and black chalk. Berlin-West, Kupferstichkabinett (KDZ 26202).

(d) *Digging for the Cross*. Paris, Louvre (Inv. 21388). Pen and coloured washes, which agree more or less with those of the painting.

(e) do., Paris, Louvre (Inv. 21088). Pen and wash.

(f) do., Düsseldorf, Kunstmuseum (Inv. FP 10168). Pen and wash, heightened with white on yellow paper.

17. Series of Saints and Figures from the Old and New Testaments. About 1605 (Plates 55–63 and Col. Plate IV)

A: St. John the Baptist	F: Tobias and the Angel
B: St. John the Evangelist	G: St Anne and the Virgin
C: St. Peter	H: St. Joseph and the Christ Child
D: St. Paul	
E: St. Thomas Aquinas	I: St. Lawrence

(A–H) National Trust (Petworth House); (I) Montpellier, Musée Fabre.

Oil on silvered copper, 90×70.

PROVENANCE: (A–H) Possibly the 'Eight little pieces' by Enson Hamor [sic] in the collection of the Duke of Buckingham at York House in 1635 (see R. Davies, in *Burlington Magazine*, 1906/7, p. 382); Duke of Northumberland, Northumberland House: 'eight little pictures in one Frame by Elshammer', appraised at £250 by Symond Stowe in the 1671 valuation of the pictures at Alnwick (this information from F. St. John Gore); by descent to Lord Leconsfield, Petworth. (I) François-Xavier Fabre; presented in 1825.

LITERATURE: Drost 1933, p. 58; W I, p. 112, figs. 42–5; W II, pp. 33 and 220.

EXHIBITIONS: (A–H) London (Wildenstein), *Pictures from Petworth House*, 1954, No. 5; Manchester, *Between Renaissance and Baroque*, 1965, Nos. 86–93. (I) Frankfurt 1966/67, No. 24, fig. 22.

These nine little panels are the surviving originals of a series which at one time must have comprised at least ten: an additional *Abraham and Isaac* is confirmed by the set of copies by Cornelis Poelenburgh in the Pitti (Pl. 64; see below). In fact the ensemble may have been even larger: a seventeenth-century Dutch cabinet in a Private Collection (see *Country Life*, 23 March 1912, p. 438) contains on its front the whole series as copied by Poelenburgh, but in addition three more panels, a standing *St. Francis*, a *Magdalen* and a *Female Saint* in a white robe with a staff over her shoulder (possibly St. Ursula). These copies are also very close to Poelenburgh's style, but may be an imitation of it. Tradition has it that this cabinet was given by James I to Robert Sidney, first Earl of Leicester. This would mean that it must have occurred before 1625, when the King, who had become James I in 1603, died. Hence these copies after a work by Elsheimer would be comparatively early ones. When opened, the cabinet reveals a model of St. Peter's tomb in silver, and the silver panel on the door, which encloses the tomb, represents a *Resurrection*. Hence Weizsäcker's supposition that the little copper panels may have been intended as decorations for a piece of furniture appears to be correct, and the original piece of furniture was possibly also of a devotional nature. The true purpose of the cabinet is disguised by additional panels of secular subjects. The original Elsheimer panels were very likely inserted straight into such a cabinet. The 'Kunstschränke', made with such skill in Augsburg and surroundings, were also made by German craftsmen in Italy at this time, or the panels could have been taken to the North and inlaid into a piece of furniture there. However, as Poelenburgh's copies were probably made in Italy, and have remained there, the originals were no doubt intended for an Italian destination.

Panel E has always been interpreted as St. Dominic, because of the habit, but I believe that it represents St. Thomas Aquinas, who entered the Dominican Order in 1243. Although not depicted with his familiar attribute (book), it would seem that the quill-pen and the model of the church he holds in his hands refer to Thomas's extensive writings (*Summa Theologica*), whilst the elaborate architectural background was possibly intended to represent the Cistercian monastery Fossanova, where he died.

Panel I (St. Lawrence) is undoubtedly the original, whereas the Karlsruhe panel (slightly larger in size), though a copy, is not weak, as Weizsäcker maintained, but of excellent quality. Only the face, hands and feet lack the crisp modelling one would expect from an Elsheimer original. It may possibly have been the painting which Sandrart reported seeing at his cousin Abraham Mertens in Frankfurt.

The thematic connection of the panels is not clear, if such a connection was intended at all. The source of the series must have been the engraved figures of Saints by Dürer and Schongauer, but perhaps also the series of Apostles engraved by Marcantonio after Raphael (B. XIV, Sp. 74, 65–76), which would imply a fusion of German and Italian influences.

The almost perfect condition of the panels (minor defects,

due to cracking and pin-poi[...]
in G and H) allows one t[...]
sublime. The Petworth seri[...]
skill by John Brealey in 1[...]
Elsheimer's inherent monu[...]
forcefully. The very free b[...]
passages, is quite unlike wha[...]
a 'miniature' painter. It wa[...]
these panels that, almost 1[...]
works, made a powerful i[...]
Elder (see his *Tobias and th*[...]
whether Claude Lorrain k[...]
(see Pl. 132).

VERSIONS: (I) *St. Lawrence*[...]
Paris 1773, II, p. 9: La Gal[...]
autre petit tableau représentar[...]
cette figure est très-spirituelle[...]
coulent semblable à celle de l[...]
(b) Sale, London, Dr. Br[...]
Lot 32: *St. Lawrence* in a [...]
landscape, in his left hand[...]
supports an olive branch.

COPIES: (A–H) Poelenburg[...]
the Private Collection me[...]
A: Anon. Pen and wa[...]
Hollandaise II, No. 942;[...]
E: Chatsworth drawing, [...]
F: Anon. seventeenth ce[...]
Kunsthaus Heylshof.
G: Anon. seventeenth ce[...]
National Portrait Gallery[...]
G: Anon. Pen and ink[...]
(Frankfurt 1966/67, No. [...]
G: Chatsworth drawing[...]
H: C. Poelenburgh. R[...]
8354) (as Breenbergh).
H: Poelenburgh (copy). [...]
Dunbrody.
H: Anon. Pen and in[...]
(Frankfurt 1966/67, No. [...]
I: Anon. seventeenth ce[...]
Kunsthalle (Frankfurt 19[...]
I: Anon. seventeenth ce[...]
Molesworth (Frankfurt [...]
I: Anon. Coll. Duke of[...]

ADAPTATIONS: Pen and[...]
D, E, F and G are in th[...]

ETCHINGS, etc.: B: Hol[...]
H: Hollar. Parthey 16[...]
W II, p. 148).
H: van Somer, Mezzo[...]
I: Hollar. Parthey 170.[...]

18. Aurora. About 16[...]
Braunschweig, Herzog[...]
Oil on copper, 170×[...]
Elsehimer fecit Romae.

PROVENANCE: Collect[...]
Salzdahlum (since 1744[...]

LITERATURE: Sandrart, p. 161; Bode 1883, p. 282; Drost 1933, p. 104; W I, p. 246, pl. 135; Holzinger 1951, p. 223; W II, p. 60, No. 59; R. Hohl, *Claude Lorrain und die barocke Landschaftszeichnung* (Diss. 1961), Basle 1972, p. 59; Knut Nicolaus, 'Elsheimers "Aurora" im Lichte naturwissenschaftlicher Untersuchungen', in *Maltechnik/Restauro 2*, 1974, p. 98.

EXHIBITIONS: *Aufgang der Neuzeit*, Nuremberg 1952, R7; *L'Ideale Classico del Seicento*, 1962, No. 121; *Deutsche Maler und Zeichner des 17. Jahrhunderts*, Berlin 1966, No. 14; Frankfurt 1966/67, No. 39, fig. 36.

Ever since Bode first discussed the painting in 1883, uneasiness has been expressed from time to time about its status. How much does the damage—especially on the left-hand side—hide of the original paint; is it an original at all; was it left unfinished and has another hand intervened, for how else can the utter magic of the rosy morning sky be reconciled with the hasty, superficial passages in the landscape? The indecision was increased by the comparison with Goudt's print of 1613 (see below). When engraving the work, back in his native Holland, Goudt almost certainly owned the painting, but it may be significant that he omitted the whole of the left-hand side, exactly that passage which is the most problematic. Even the naked eye can here discern damage, overpaint and a totally different craquelure from the rest of the picture. Knut Nicolaus, the restorer at the Braunschweig Museum, revealed by scientific means in a fascinating study that the striding herdsman is an overpainting and that underneath are several other figures, though of twice the size as the herdsman (roughly on the scale of the figures in the *Large Tobias*) as well as a Cyclops-like head at the top of the protruding tree. What the explanation is to be, whether the story of Acis and Galatea was intended and then abandoned, must remain conjectural. In any case it seems clear that Holzinger's interpretation of the subject being Cephalus and Procris has to be abandoned.

It seems likely that Elsheimer left the painting unfinished and that Goudt 'filled in' the missing passages and possibly also went over some details in the middle distance which look superficially executed.

The hills and the tower-like building are reminiscent of the Villa of Maecenas and the Anio Valley below Tivoli. This is Elsheimer's most 'Virgilian' landscape, and the delicate sunlight with which it is suffused became important for artists such as Hercules Segers and Jan van der Velde (*Vesper*).

DRAWING: The drawing in Berlin (Cat. 42), though not a preliminary drawing in the strictest sense, is connected with the composition of the *Aurora*.

COPY: Goudt(?), pen and ink and brush. Frankfurt, Städelsches Kunstinstitut (Inv. 5488), part of the Frankfurt 'Klebeband'. This is not, as so many have suggested, a preliminary study for the *Aurora* (M.67), looking forward as far as Poussin in its technique, but an imitation, 'à la Elsheimer' by Goudt, as Hohl had also recognized.

ENGRAVINGS: Goudt (Pl. 67). 128×169. Signed and inscribed: HGoudt Palat. Comes, et Aur. Mil.Eques. 1613. Two states are known.
Lucas Vorsterman, Copy after Goudt's print. 2 states, before and after letters.

VERSION: Possibly 'A small landscape, sunrise, with figures; the parting of Diana from Endymion—a sweet gem'. Sale, Christie (W. Comyns), 6 May 1815, Lot 18, bought Hilder £14 14s.

19. Il Contento. About 1607 (Plate 71)
Edinburgh, National Gallery of Scotland (Inv. 2312).
Oil on copper, 301×420.

PROVENANCE: Inventory 1610, fol. 861r: *Un Rame dove è dipinto Il dio del Contento con molte figure non finito*; possibly in collection of Cardinal Odoardo Farnese, 1615 (see Andrews, p. 19); du Fay, Frankfurt 1666–1734; till 1780 M. Poullain, Receveur Général des Domaines du Roi, Paris; Poullain Sale, Paris, 20 March 1781, Lot 21; bought Langlier; Richard Payne Knight, Downton Castle; then by descent to Major Kincaid Lennox; acquired in lieu of death duties by the National Gallery of Scotland, 1970.

LITERATURE: Sandrart, p. 161; W I, pp. 146 ff., 246; W II, pp. 55 f.; E. K. Waterhouse, in *Burlington Magazine*, 1953, p. 306; J. I. Kuznetsow, in *Oud Holland*, vol. 79, 1964, pp. 229 f.; K. Andrews, *Il Contento*, 1971 (with full bibliography); Hohl, 1973, p. 188.

EXHIBITIONS: *Art Treasures of the Midlands*, Birmingham 1934, No. 132, as 'The destruction of the Idols'; *Works of Art from Midland Houses*, Birmingham 1953, No. 146; *Artists in Seventeenth Century Rome*, London (Wildenstein), 1955, No. 43; *German Art*, Manchester 1961, No. 158; Frankfurt 1966/67, No. 42.

The painting was in Elsheimer's studio at the time of his death—unfinished. That parts of the foreground figures and parts of the middle distance had been gone over by another, though contemporary, hand was recognized before the Inventory, which proves this, had been discovered (Andrews, p. 13). After having been given the most unlikely titles, the painting's real theme was first pointed out by Kuznetsow. It has been taken from an interpolated narrative in Alemán's picaresque novel *Guzman de Alfarache*, first published in Madrid in 1599 (Italian translation 1606). It tells of Jupiter's anger at the self-indulgence of the people and their neglect in worshipping the gods. At his behest, Mercury abducts the goddess Content, which the people try and prevent. The story can be traced to classical and Renaissance authors: Lucian, Alberti, Doni (Andrews, pp. 2–3). Sandrart, who knew the correct title of the painting, considered it to be Elsheimer's masterpiece and it is certainly his most elaborate composition.

Hohl has proposed a Roman relief as the source for the composition of the foreground which is, however, not very convincing. Much closer is in fact an engraving by Cornelis Cort of a Roman sacrificial procession (Pl. 112) after Lambert Lombard (Bierens de Haan 90–91). (Lombard's original drawing, in two sections like the engraving, is in Berlin, KDZ 12271-2). Several details, such as the man with outstretched arms, the woman with the child, as well as other single figures and the sacrificial animals have close parallels in Elsheimer's painting.

The background of the picture shows the people preoccupied with sports and games, whilst Jupiter fulminates in front of a temple on the left, at the moment when Mercury abducts the goddess. The entrance of the temple is covered by an elaborate tapestry, showing an Emperor on horseback with his equerry (in sixteenth-century costume), whilst at the extreme left, on another hanging, we see a King or Emperor being crowned, and below him is displayed the emblem of the double eagle, the insignia of the Hapsburg monarchs. The curious insertion of contemporary symbolism into classical events can only be explained as intending a juxtaposition of temporal and divine power, in terms which would have been understood by a contemporary spectator. It might be recalled that very similar figures (the Pope and Emperor) with the Hapsburg emblem and the Fleur-de-lis occur in Bosch's *Haywain* (Prado), where the divine power is Christ, not Jupiter. See also *Juno* (Cat. 22c).

ENGRAVING: Pierre Antoine Martini (when in the collection of Poullain). Andrews, fig. 9.

PRELIMINARY DRAWINGS: see Cat. 43, 44 and 45.

COPIES: (a) Anon. Pen and wash. Utrecht, Coll. Dr. Ingrid van Gelder-Jost (Andrews, fig. 6). It shows the composition as Elsheimer left it.
(b) Anon. Pen and wash (Pl. 119). Coll. M. C. Naumann (Andrews, fig. 7). Inscribed and dated ANNO MDCXV A ROMA. It shows the 'completed' composition.
(c) Anon. Pen and wash. Vienna, Albertina (Andrews, fig. 8). E. Haverkamp Begemann, *Willem Buytewech*, Amsterdam 1959, p. 36 suggests an attribution to Uyttenbroeck.
(d) Johann König. Watercolour on vellum. Munich, Residenz (Andrews, fig. 10).
(e) Possibly Inventory Jeremias Wildens (30 Dec. 1653) *Een Copie, synde een Offerande naer Elshamer, No. 643*, J. Denucé, *Konstkamers*, p. 168.

ADAPTATIONS: (f) N. Knüpfer (Pl. 120). Munich, Alte Pinakothek (Andrews, fig. 13).
(g) P. P. Rubens (left portion of the painting; Pl. 122). London, Coll. Count Antoine Seilern (Andrews, fig. 11).
(h) N. Knüpfer (Pl. 121). Schwerin, Staatliches Museum. A freer composition of the same subject (Andrews, fig. 14).
(i) Willem van Nieuland II, whereabouts unknown (Andrews, fig. 12).
(j) Adriaen van Stalbemt, Basle, Öffentliche Kunstsammlung (Andrews, fig. 15).

20. Tobias and the Angel (The Small Tobias). About 1607–8 (Plate 72)
Frankfurt, Historisches Museum (Inv. B 789).
Oil on copper, 124 × 192 (plate); 116 × 184 (composition).

PROVENANCE: Possibly Johann Jakob Schmitz (1724–96), because the portrait of his wife shows her holding the painting in her hand, though it is not certain whether this is in fact the Frankfurt picture (see *Katalog der Deutschen Gemälde von 1550 bis 1800 im Wallraf-Richartz Museum*, Köln, 1973, No. 1096, fig. 92); K. L. Goedecker, Mainz; acquired 1886.

LITERATURE: Sandrart, p. 160; W I, p. 120; F. Bothe, *Adam Elsheimer der Maler von Frankfurt*, 1939, pp. 86–7; W II, p. 12, Cat. 8; Holzinger 1951, p. 210; W. Prinz, *Gemälde des Historischen Museums Frankfurt*, 1957, p. 90; Waddingham 1972, p. 610.

EXHIBITIONS: *Deutsche Me[...] hunderts*, Berlin 1966, No. [...] fig. 5.

According to Sandrart, this [...] Elsheimer famous in Ron[...] original painting or Goud[...] the first he made after Elsh[...] print is dated 1608, and t[...] *Mocking of Ceres* (1610), th[...] Elsheimer painting.

The two serious contest[...] been the Frankfurt paintin[...] Daan Cevat. I agree with[...] Frankfurt painting and w[...] might be the original by [...] correspond with Goudt's[...] version they do not, b[...] Elsheimer) visible in those[...] thin, the livelier handling[...] as well as the handling of[...] its being an original. Adr[...] looks unusual for Elshein[...] tion.

The story of Tobias a[...] for apart from the so-[...] depicted the scene in or[...] and in a gouache at Berl[...] not only engraved ag[...] Elsheimer's followers, s[...] inspired by the maste[...] version (Coll. F. Lugt, [...]

ENGRAVINGS: (a) Hend[...] states known, of which [...] in the British Museum) [...]
(b) W. Hollar. Etching [...]
(c) Carl Agricola (1812[...]
(d) Cornelis Galle. Co[...]
(e) John Lloyd. Mezzo[...]
(f) John Smith. Mezzo[...]

COPIES: The majority [...] Weizsäcker have not b[...] examples, unknown to[...]
(g) Coll. Daan Cevat. [...] Fonthill Abbey 1844; [...] Hon. W. Massey-Ma[...] Martin; Daan Cevat [...] Lot 68; unsold). *Exh[...] London (Wildenstein[...] No. 4, fig. 4.
(h) Coll. Margery Gr[...] Lost, but said to have[...] seventeenth century.
(i) Coll. Schwalbe, [...] version now at the P[...]
(j) Pushkin Museum [...] (Ill. Drost 1933, fig. [...]
(k) Coll. Dr. Alfred [...]
(l) Lasson Gallery, L[...] after Goudt.

(m) Gallery J. Kugel, Paris (1973). Panel, 130×195. ? eighteenth century.

(n) Amsterdam, Gallery P. de Boer, April 1976. Copper, 220×295. With variations in the landscape.

(o) Drawing, pen and ink, in the 'Klebeband' of the Strasbourg painter Friedrich Brentel at Karlsruhe (F6/18). Copy after Goudt.

(p) Windsor, Royal Collection (Inv. 6300). Pen and wash. The drawing shows elements of both the Small and the Large Tobias and may well be by Claes Moeyaert.

ADAPTATION: (q) Buyewtech. Drawing. British Museum (Inv. 1805.5.9.1891). Landscape taken from Goudt's engraving.

21. **Apollo and Coronis.** About 1607-8 (Plate 76)
Corsham Court, Lord Methuen.
Oil on copper, 174×216.

PROVENANCE: Sir Paul Methuen (1672-1757); bequeathed to his cousin Paul Methuen; Paul Methuen collection, Grosvenor Street, London; then Corsham House; Sale, Christie, 13 May 1920, Lot 17; bought back by Lord Methuen.

LITERATURE: Sandrart, p. 160; (T. Martyn) *The English Connoisseur*, 1766, I, p. 31; G. F. Waagen, *Works of Art and Artists in England*, 1838, III, p. 105; Bode 1883, p. 294; Drost 1933, p. 85; W I, p. 140, pl. 71; W II, pp. 46-7 (all these as 'Death of Procris'); Holzinger 1951, p. 216.

EXHIBITIONS: The British Institution, 1857, No. 102; *Seventeenth Century Art*, London (Royal Academy), 1938, No. 257; *Artists in Seventeenth Century Rome*, London (Wildenstein), 1955, No. 42; Frankfurt 1966/67, No. 35.

Ever since Magdalena de Passe's engraving, the subject has been interpreted as *The Death of Procris*. Holzinger recognized the true theme, taken from the *Metamorphoses* of Ovid, II, 542: the death of Coronis, who had been unfaithful to Apollo and was killed by him with an arrow in an act of jealousy. The god immediately regretted his deed and hoped to save her life by looking for healing herbs. But it is too late, the funeral pyre is being prepared and all Apollo can do is wrest the unborn child (Aesculapius) from her womb.

The figure of Coronis may be a recollection from Titian, possibly the nude female figure in the *Bacchanal* (*The Andrians*), which was in the Aldobrandini collection in Rome between 1598 and 1621 and could thus have been seen by Elsheimer. (The other painting which comes to mind, *Jupiter and Antiope* (Louvre), had been in Spain since 1564.)

Few compositions by Elsheimer have been copied so frequently. Weizsäcker (W II, p. 47) prints a long list, of which the majority cannot now be traced. For those which merit consideration, see below. In spite of damages, which Waagen already noticed, the version at Corsham Court is likely to be the original. It differs in minor details from de Passe's engraving, but then it is not known which was her prototype. The Corsham painting was cleaned by J. Hell in 1949. There are damages along the lower margins and the rather hard cloud seems to have been overpainted. The flecks of light among the foliage are colour and not, as might be thought, tinned copper shining through, and may originally

have been softened by glazes, such as are still visible on Apollo's head.

ENGRAVINGS: (a) Magdalena de Passe, with inscription *Adam Elsheimer pinxit.*
(b) do. The same figure as Coronis, but with arrow and more drapery. Apollo (?) behind bushes. No figure on the left, but a gate and a hound. (Impression in the Albertina HB51, No. 23.)

DERIVATION: A drawing by Daniel Verstangen, a pupil of Poelenburgh, in Hamburg (Inv. 22642) of the same subject.

VERSIONS: (a) Coll. Georg Schäfer, Obbach nr. Schweinfurt (W II, No. 49a). Copper, 178×230. Coll.: De Vigny (Architecte du Roi), Paris 1773; The Rt. Hon. Charles Seale Hayne; Sir Claude Phillips; Lady Martin; Leonard Koetser, Exh. April–May 1962, No. 16. Excellent quality, though some of the middle-ground figures are too bland for Elsheimer. (The Schäfer collection also includes another, but very inferior copy.)
(b) Coll. Lt. Col. J. H. S. Lucas-Scudamore, Kentchurch Court, Hereford. Copper, 178×231. Coll.: Sir Harford Jones-Brydges. Exh.: *Works of Art from Midland Houses*, Birmingham 1953, No. 147. Also of excellent quality, especially in the landscape background and the foliage. But the draperies on which Coronis reclines are too superficially modelled for an original Elsheimer. Also the features of Coronis and the satyrs in the middle-distance have not the typical Elsheimer physiognomies.
(c) Yale University Art Gallery, New Haven (Inv. 1956.17.1). Copper, 178×235. Coll. Dr. A. Jaffé, Berlin (W II, p. 48, No. 49c).
(d) Coll. Mrs. Kate Schaeffer, New York. Copper, 178×226. (Frankfurt Exh. 1966/67, No. 36.)
(e) Frankfurt, Historisches Museum. Copper, 175×229. (Frankfurt Exh. 1966/67, No. 37.)
(f) Coll. Dr. Dieter Gescher, Neuilly, France. Copper, 178×228. Probably of a later date than the above, c. 1660-70. Exhibited at the Frankfurt 1966/67 exhibition, but not in the catalogue.

22. **The Three Realms of the World.** About 1607-8 (Plates 77-81)
(a) The Realm of Venus.
(b) The Realm of Minerva.
Cambridge, Fitzwilliam Museum. Inv. 532 and 539.
Oil on copper, 87×146.
(c) The Realm of Juno.
Only known through the etching by Hollar. 90×170.

PROVENANCE: Thomas Howard, Earl of Arundel; (a) and (b): Robert Grave; Sale, Christie, 12 May 1827, Lot 42; bought Daniel Messman; bequeathed to the Fitzwilliam Museum 1834.

LITERATURE: Bode 1883, p. 291; Drost 1933, p. 92; W I, pp. 115, 136; W II, p. 52; Fitzwilliam Museum: Catalogue of Paintings, I, 1960, p. 201; G. Krämer, 'Das Kompositionsprinzip bei Adam Elsheimer', in *Städel Jahrbuch*, N.F., IV, 1973, p. 156.

EXHIBITION: (c) Frankfurt 1966/67, No. 284, fig. 175.

Of the three panels two have survived. The third is only

known from Hollar's etching, made when all three were in the Arundel collection. It is likely that they were intended to be let into a piece of furniture. It is interesting to observe, as Krämer has also pointed out, that none of the figures (which the Vienna version of the *Venus* 'corrected') is aligned along the vertical middle axis, but all are slightly off-centre. In both the Cambridge pictures, the paint has darkened considerably and in the *Venus* panel the two main figures and passages in the sky are damaged, possibly by previous overcleaning and repainting.

The *Minerva* appears to have had some influence on Moeyaert's design for the title-page of Jacob Struyd's tragedy *Albonus en Rosimonda* (Amsterdam 1631).

The *Juno* is seen seated in front of a tapestry which, as in *Il Contento*, shows an emperor or king, again possibly emblems of divine and temporal power. It is very likely that Rembrandt knew Hollar's etching of this figure, for his own painting of *Juno* (recently acquired by Dr. Armand Hammer, until then on loan to the Metropolitan Museum, New York) is quite close in conception to that of Elsheimer.

ENGRAVINGS: (a) Hollar, 1646 (Parthey 270–2). Etchings (Pls. 79–81).
(b) Johanna Sibylla Küslen (1646–1717). Copies from Hollar, in reverse.
(c) N. Donne (second half of eighteenth century). *Venus*. Copy from Hollar in reverse.
(d) L. Vorsterman. *Venus*. In the same sense as the Cambridge picture.

COPY: (a) *Venus*. Vienna, Gemäldegalerie der Akademie der Bildenden Künste (Inv. 726). Copper, 94×151 (Pl. 126). Definitely a copy of the Cambridge picture, but in better condition.

23. The Mocking of Ceres. About 1608 (Plate 82)
Madrid, Museo del Prado (Inv. 2181).
Oil on copper, 295×241.

PROVENANCE: ? Cornelis van der Geest (Denucé, p. 53: 1638 'Elsheimer. Ceres en Stellio'); Peter Paul Rubens (Inventory 1640, No. 32: Denucé, p. 58: 'Une Cérès á la nuit, d'Adam Elshamer'); also 1645 (Denucé, p. 75) 'Een stuck van Ceres in de nacht'; bought 1645 for King Philip IV of Spain; since 1686 in the Inventory of the Alcazar, Madrid.

LITERATURE: Sandrart, p. 161; Drost 1933, p. 80, pl. x; W I, p. 183, pl. 93; W II, p. 41, Cat. 42; G. Krämer, 'Das Kompositionsprinzip bei Adam Elsheimer', in *Städel Jahrbuch*, N.F., IV, 1973, p. 157.

EXHIBITIONS: *Deutsche Maler und Zeichner des 17. Jahrhunderts*, Berlin 1966, No. 12; Frankfurt 1966/67, No. 32, fig. 30.

The theme is taken from Ovid, *Metamorphoses*, v, 446–61, which describes how Ceres, searching for her abducted daughter Proserpine, arrives at the hut of an old woman and asks for a drink of water. Whilst she drinks greedily, she is mocked by the young boy Stellio, whom she angrily transforms into a lizard. The story of Ceres fascinated Elsheimer and he treated the subject several times (see Cat. 50 and 51).

As in the case of the *Large Tobias*, the original painting by Elsheimer, from which Goudt made his engraving (Pl. 86),

has been lost. The Prado
Rubens's collection, cannot
painting is far too bland an
of the Old Woman and th
Ceres and the two figures
The best passages are the wh
and flowers on the left. Rul
previous scholars into insis
be an original Elsheimer, as
a workshop copy from hi
1966 Catalogue). Howeve
letter of January 1611 tha
Flanders then owned any o
Hence the picture now in t
the North after 1611. It is
Rubens's possession, it bel
in whose collection a versi
on the right, in Willem va
Regent's visit to the picture
Rubenshuis), dated 1628.
must have come into Ru
date of van der Geest's in
der Geest collection and i
shown in profile whereas
at the spectator. As all
Elsheimer compositions
assumed that the origina
recorded in Goudt's pri
statement that the Prad
original, but had been o
would explain the discre
and Goudt's print. There
painting or of a second h
sections of the Prado pai
obviously by a contempo
that quite soon after Elsh
attached to copies and i
John at Munich, Pl. 113)

It is curious that some
the Prado painting, whi
as in Goudt's print. It i
experimented with the in
In fact, in a London pr
discovered painting on
characteristic grey und
before it was finished
Although some passage
those in the Prado pictu
manner, it cannot but b
that the copyist experim
boy's head (he attempte
a third leg. What the st
experiments and their
remains a puzzle. Perha
copies may point to tw
existed. Whatever the
work made a great imp
The most unexpected
in a book by Elsheime
animals, whose full titl

medici et professoris Romani, et jam quinque Summis Pontificibus ab herbariis studiis, Animalia Mexicana descriptionibus scholiisque exposita. Thesauri rerum medicarum Novae Hispaniae seu plantarum . . . Rome, 1628 (second edition 1651). When Faber comes to discuss and describe the Mexican lizard 'Stellio Novae Hispaniae' (p. 748), he says:

'Even if asked to judge, I shall be loth to give my verdict on who has provided the more elegant version of this tale—Ovid, that most eloquent poet, or Adam Elsheimer of Frankfurt, once a regular guest in my house, with his most charming painting. He painted this story on a copper plate one and a half spans long and one wide, with such skill and artistry, such learning and talent and allowed it thereafter to be engraved on copper, that no comparable work of art had ever been seen at Rome and on that account it was sold for more than two hundred gold Philippes. Here, where small figures had to be represented as though living and breathing, and at night-time too, or at sunrise or sunset, where rain-showers, tides or some such natural phenomenon had to be depicted and painted, he took the palm above all painters of his time. In rendering the charm of woods and trees, the beauty of flowers, the pleasures of the countryside in living colour, he so captured the true essence of nature that he opened the eyes of painters not only of his own day but (in this matter especially) of those too who came after. Only the late Paul Bril of Belgium, a painter of great distinction at Rome, could teach this. After he followed Adam's manner, in these last twenty years of his life, he left us works in this kind of painting (the Italians call them 'Paesi') which are really golden; but those which he himself gave to the world before these twenty years are of bronze (if I may say so), although he was famous even then. But, these are only words, you will say. So I invite you to view Adam's works themselves; I have some, though only a few, at home.'

ENGRAVING: (a) Hendrick Goudt, dated 1610, with dedication to Cardinal Scipio Borghese (Pl. 86). A hitherto unknown First State, before the fine shading in some of the dark areas, was sold at Craddock & Barnard, London, Cat. 128, December 1973, No. 74. (Friedrich Noack, in his manuscript-notes, now in the Bibliotheca Hertziana, Rome, states that Goudt started the engraving in January 1610, but without revealing his source).

COPIES: (b) J. Rutgers. Copy after Goudt (in reverse).
(c) In the sense of the Prado painting: London, Private Collection. Measurements are the same as those of the Prado picture (see above).
(d) In the sense of Goudt's engraving: Braunschweig, Herzog-Anton-Ulrich Museum. Copper, 310×240. *Exh.*: Frankfurt 1966/67, No. 33, fig. 31.
(e) Zürich, Kurt Meissner. Copper. Early seventeenth century.
(f) Berlin, Schloss Grunewald. Copper.
(g) Gateshead, Dr. F. Binder. Copper.
(h) Drawing: Rome, Gabinetto Disegni (Inv. F.C.1511, vol. 157, G.1).

DERIVATIONS: (i) Hendrick Bary (fl. 1626-75). Engraving,

as 'after Elsheimer', though a totally different composition (Hollstein 6).
(j) B. Capitelli. Etching. 1633. (B. XX, p. 159, 25.)
(k) A. de Grebber. Painting on panel. Signed. (Photo, Rijksbureau, The Hague, No. L.7083.)
(l) Jan van de Velde. Engraving. 'L'etoile des Rois' (Nagler 47).
(m) L. Bramer, *Stellio changed into a lizard*. Drawing. Coll. Mr. and Mrs. Julius Held (Exh. Cat. Binghampton 1970, No. 23).
(n) Jacob Jordaens (Studio). Painting. Bourges, Musée du Berry.
(o) *Proserpine in search of her daughter, a young boy turned into a lizard by the old woman* [sic], offered by John Hamilton Reid in a letter to W. F. Skene, Secretary to the Royal Institution, Edinburgh, 30 January 1856.

24. **Jupiter and Mercury in the House of Philemon and Baucis.** About 1608-9 (Plate 87)
Dresden, Staatliche Kunstsammlungen, Gemäldegalerie (Inv. 1977).
Oil on copper, 169×224.

PROVENANCE: Hendrick Goudt (by 1612); (possibly Coll. Johan van de Capelle. Inv. 13 August 1680, No. 52 'een Philemon en Baucis van Elzhamer'; Sale, Grave van Wassenaar d'Obdam, den Haag, 19 August 1750, Lot 104, *Jupiter en Mercurius, bij Philemon en Baucis, door Adam Elshamer. h.6½ d., br.9 d.*, bt. Huistenray, fl. 305.-); first recorded in the Dresden Gallery in 1754.

LITERATURE: Sandrart, p. 161; Drost 1933, pp. 94-5, pl. XII; W I, p. 195, pl. 98; Holzinger 1951, p. 209; W II, p. 42, Cat. No. 43; K. Bauch, *Der frühe Rembrandt und seine Zeit*, 1960, p. 131.

EXHIBITION: Frankfurt 1966/67, No. 38, fig. 35.

The incident depicted, a rather rare subject in the visual arts before Elsheimer, has been taken from Ovid, who describes (*Metamorphoses*, VIII, 618-724) how the two gods found shelter in the humble hut of the old couple.

The provenance given above, with the exception of the first and last items, is conjectural, as the painting in J. van de Capelle's collection could also have been the one later in Lely's collection (which was of the same size as the Dresden painting, but cannot be that picture, as Lely's can be traced in England till 1834—see below). It must be considered certain that it was in Goudt's possession when he made his engraving from it in 1612 (Pl. 88) and that he took it with him from Rome when he returned to Utrecht after Elsheimer's death. However, it is likely that the work was finished by the end of 1608, for Rubens—who returned to Antwerp from Rome in October of that year—must have known the painting, for it (rather than Goudt's print) influenced passages—and especially the old woman—in such works as *The Adoration of the Shepherds* (Edinburgh, National Gallery of Scotland) and *Philopoemen recognized by an old woman* (Louvre).

Stylistically, the Dresden painting is close to the *Ceres* (moreover, the old woman and the figure of Baucis are obviously the same model or the same idea) and to the

Minerva, in which the seated scholar with the globe prefigures the Jupiter.

The condition of the picture is good on the whole. There is some slight damage and overpaint on Jupiter's cloak, on that of Baucis and on the goose in the foreground; the typical grey underpainting is visible in the figure of Baucis.

ENGRAVING: Hendrick Goudt (Pl. 88). Signed and dated 1612 (without mention of Elsheimer's name).

COPIES: (a) Sir Peter Lely, Sale, 18 April 1682 (Brit. Mus. Add. MSS. 23081, 74–8), No. 70: 'Elsheimer: a curious small piece being the history of Philemon and Baucis. 6¾ in.× 8¾ in.; bought (1683) by Anthony, Earl of Kent, for £76 for the 'curious small piece'; Thomas Philip Earl de Grey, Catalogue of Pictures . . . at his house, St. James's Square, 1834. No. 54. Elsheimer, the story of Baucis and Philemon. On copper, 6¾ inches high, 8¾ inches wide.'

(b) Weizsäcker (W II, p. 43) refers to a version in the collection Henneberg at Zürich, which was auctioned by Helbing in Munich in 1903, but bought in.

25. Tobias and the Angel (The large Tobias). About 1609
(Plate 89)
Copenhagen, Statens Museum for Kunst (Inv. Sp.745).
Oil on copper, 210×270.

PROVENANCE: G. Morell; acquired by the Museum in 1760.

LITERATURE: Catalogue Statens Museum for Kunst, 1951, No. 207; W II, p. 13, No. 9.

EXHIBITION: Frankfurt 1966/67, No. 7, fig. 6.

Elsheimer's original painting of this subject, which no doubt was in Goudt's possession when he made his engraving from it in 1613 (Pl. 90), has been lost. It seems to me that the version at Copenhagen, though a contemporary copy, comes nearer to Elsheimer's style—and to Goudt's engraving—than the better known one in the National Gallery in London (Pl. 123). The latter (at one time in William Beckford's collection) has been accepted as a damaged original by Bode, Davies and Levey; Weizsäcker expressed doubts but accepted it as a studio work; Sir Walter Armstrong thought it was by Claes Moeyaert; whilst Drost suggested an attribution to Roos. The last two ideas seem to be nearer the truth as far as date is concerned, for the London painting appears not far from the copies which David Teniers the Younger made after earlier masters, and thus the picture should be dated in the 1650s. It is painted on an unusually thick copper plate which had previously been used for an engraving of some stylized heraldic patterns and of a chain with a Maltese Cross, which can be seen if the surface of the plate is tilted against the light.

The Copenhagen painting, though closer to Elsheimer in style and composition, is rather tightly painted, in the manner of Johann König, though I would hesitate to attribute the picture to him. The composition agrees with that depicted in Goudt's print, which the London version does not. Stylistically, the work appears to be a late one, close to the *Ceres* and looking forward to the *Flight into Egypt*.

ENGRAVINGS: (a) Hendrick Goudt (Pl. 90). 1613. 197×256. Lucas Vorsterman. Copy after Goudt (but the figures only). (Hercules Segers made an etching in adaptation of Goudt's

print (Haverkamp Begeman
Rembrandt's possession, who
into Egypt (B.56) and change

VERSIONS: (b) Carel de Moc
VI, p. 2180; W II, p. 223), 1
of fl. 700 to Laurens van d'
over koop van zeker stuck sc
van Elshamer. Sale (Lord Sp
1811, Lot 272 'Tobit and th
clear whether this was the c
Tobias. London, National
193×276. For full discussio
Michael Levey, *National*
School, 1959, p. 40.

COPY: (c) Basle, Robert v
Coll.: W. Esdaile. (Möhle
Goudt's print with some
the Large Tobias. Like the
this may be by Gerrit van

26. The Flight into Egy
Munich, Alte Pinakothek
Oil on copper, 310×410
Elsheimer fecit Romae 1609.

PROVENANCE: Elsheimer
Hendrick Goudt (who e
who is said to have sh
Elector Maximilian I of B
(1628), No. 17: *Ein andre*
hoch, darauf von gedachten
die nacht gemalt ist. (Inve
Stückken, auch vornemmen
zue finden sind. Munich,
by inheritance to Elector
Düsseldorf and Mannhei

LITERATURE: Sandrart, p
to Dr. Johannes Faber (I
1933, p. 112; W I, p. 2
Stechow, *Dutch Landscap*
1966, p. 174; K. Andrew
'Elsheimer and Galileo',
p. 139; K. Andrews,
Magazine, August 1976,

EXHIBITIONS: *Aufgang*
Il Seicento Europeo, Ron
No. 9, fig. 8.

The painting was in E
death, as the Inventory
Goudt back to Utrecht,
in 1613 (Pl. 92). How it
Maximilian is not clear
it must have been sold
p. 597).

That it is one of Els
creations has always be
phere which pervades t
ing of the starry sky a

first time this had appeared in a painting in a naturalistic manner. It had been suggested before (Weizsäcker, Möhle) that this feature was due to the influence of contemporary scientific writings by Kepler and Galileo. Anna Cavina Ottani put forward the suggestion that without Galileo's observation of the Milky Way through the telescope Elsheimer could not have painted this conglomeration of stars the way he did. Apart from the discrepancy of the dates (the inscription on the back of the Munich painting is 1609, whilst Galileo did not make his observation until the following year) Galileo only confirmed what had been common consent among astronomers and could, moreover, be seen by the naked eye, especially in a southern region. Furthermore, what Elsheimer depicted—the bright moon which would make the Milky Way invisible, the clouds above it, the Great Bear in the wrong position—does not point to an artist who was out to incorporate the latest scientific data into his pictures. Although it is not clear from the position of the full moon over the horizon whether the view is towards the east (evening scene) or the west (morning scene) —the former is more likely. In neither case could the Milky Way take up the position relative to the horizon as shown in the painting. In short, what Elsheimer intended to convey was an evocation, not observable scientific facts.

The panel is on the whole in excellent condition. There are some slight damages on the trees behind Joseph and retouches between the legs of that figure, as well as in the passage of the lake. Also the reflection of the moon in the water has been retouched.

ENGRAVING: Hendrick Goudt (Pl. 92). Dated 1613 (Hollstein 3).

COPIES AND ADAPTATIONS: (a) Inv. Herman de Neyt, Delft, 1642: Een vliedinge naer Egipten, naer Elshaemer, genombreert No. 98. (Denucé, Konstkamers, p. 96.)
(b) Paris, Louvre (Inv. 2710). Panel. (Pl. 124.) From coll. Prince de Conti in 1793, and probably identical with the copper, said to be by Paul Bril ('manière d'Adam') registered as No. 240 by Le Brun in the inventory of Louis XIV of 1683. This version is very close to the Munich painting, but omits the elaborate starry sky. (Exh. Frankfurt 1966/67, No. 10, fig. 9.) (Engraved by Aldenvang, after Marchis.)
(c) Innsbruck, Museum Ferdinandeum (Inv. 799).
(d) Nantes (Inv. 541). Canvas.
(e) Copenhagen, Private Collection.
(f) Florence, Coll. Ignatius Hugford (1774), according to Passavant (W II, p. 19).
(g) Norwich, Sir Edmund Bacon, Bt. Copper. Exh. Ideal and Classical Landscape, Cardiff, 1960, No. 39, as Elsheimer.
(h) Rotterdam, Museum Boymans–van Beuningen. Panel. From the coll. v.d. Vroom. Attributed to Moeyaert, but possibly by Jacob Pynas.
(i) W. Baur. Miniature drawing. Paris, Louvre (Demonts II, No. 458). Basically the same composition as (g).

INFLUENCES: (j) Rubens. Kassel. Dated 1614. (Pl. 133.)
(k) Rembrandt. Dublin. Dated 1647. (Pl. 136.)
(l) Claude Lorrain. British Museum. Drawing (Röthlisberger, No. 70). Nocturnal Landscape. c. 1635-45. Same accents of the landscape, but in reverse, so that Goudt's engraving was very likely the source.

(m) Buytewech, Ignis (etched by Jan van der Velde), Buytewech's original drawing formerly in coll. Jaremitsch. Leningrad (Haverkamp Begemann, Cat. 23, fig. 139), shows the scene in daylight, whilst v.d. Velde's etching has moonlight.
(n) Jan van de Velde, Le Soir. Engraving ('Petites planches'), has details from Elsheimer's painting.

26A. **Self-Portrait.** About 1606–7 (Plate 97)
Florence, Uffizi (Inv. 1784).
Oil on canvas, 637 × 480.

PROVENANCE: Probably the painting in Elsheimer's studio at the time of his death (see Inventory, fol. 865v); probably in the Accademia di San Luca, Rome; Cardinal Leopoldo de' Medici; first mentioned in the Uffizi inventory of 1704.

LITERATURE: Baglione, Le Vite . . . etc., 1642, p. 101; W I, pp. 92 f. and frontispiece; W II, pp. 84 f. Cat. 83; K. Andrews, 'Elsheimer's Portrait', in Album Amicorum J. G. van Gelder, The Hague, 1973, pp. 1 ff.

EXHIBITION: Frankfurt 1966/67, No. 54, fig. 46.

Most scholars have suggested that this portrait is the work of a contemporary, possibly Northern, artist. However, it can be argued (Andrews, op. cit.) that it is in fact a self-portrait, and moreover the one listed among the contents of Elsheimer's house after his death. It was probably intended for incorporation into the series of members' portraits in the Accademia di San Luca. Such a destination would also explain the—for Elsheimer—unusual format, size and support, which however conform to the other portraits in the collection. Baglione mentions a portrait of Elsheimer in the Accademia: il suo ritratto nell'Accademia di S. Luca, per eternare la sua memoria, si vede. However, the one which is now in the Academy (Pl. 99) is an inferior copy, freely based on the Uffizi painting, and its only virtue is that it bears the date 1606, which must be the year of Elsheimer's election as a member. How the original disappeared from the Academy is not clear, but it is known that some of the portraits were sold by the middle of the seventeenth century, and this may well have been among them. When it entered the Medici collection of artist's self-portraits is also not known; it is first listed there in 1704.

Although the portrait is difficult to compare with other paintings by Elsheimer (no other portraits by him are known), it shows one highly characteristic device which occurs frequently in his works: the silhouetting of the shadow-side of a figure or face by means of light (in this instance the left side). Furthermore, the pose and the concentrated, intense glance of the eyes, the very low positioning of the hand holding the palette, seem typical indications of a self-portrait.

The Uffizi portrait must also have been the source of the engraving by Hendrick Hondius (Pl. 98), which was included in his Pictorum aliquot celebrium praecipue Germaniae inferioris effigies, published in The Hague c. 1610 (the year of Elsheimer's death). On this in turn Hollar based his etching (Pl. 100), and there are copies by later artists, such as the drawing in the Uffizi by G. D. Ferretti (Inv. 5963F) which in turn was engraved by Johann Jacob Frei (cf. W II, p. 133).

DRAWINGS

27. Fama. About 1596 (Plate 2)
Karlsruhe, Staatliche Kunsthalle (Inv. VIII 2676, fol. 57, in 'Klebeband' K).
Pen and wash, 150×91. Inscribed:

> *Der Mehr nach Kunst und Ehren stelt*
> *Dann nach dem Reichtumb dieser Weltt,*
> *Desselben Lob wirdt aller Zeit*
> *Von der Fama weitt ausgebreitet.*
> *Adam Ehlsheimer*

(Who strives more after art and honour
than after the riches of this world,
his praise will at all times
be widely disseminated by Fame.)

PROVENANCE: Friedrich Brentel; possibly collection Margrave Frederick V of Baden-Durlach.

LITERATURE: Drost 1933, p. 119; W I, pp. 47, 265, pl. 4; W II, pp. 130, 158; Drost 1957, p. 117; Möhle 166, p. 111, No. 2, pl. 2; W. Wegner, 'Untersuchungen zu Friedrich Brentel', in *Jahrbuch der Staatlichen Kunstsammlungen in Baden-Württemberg*, III, 1966, p. 169, No. 50 (13).

EXHIBITION: Frankfurt 1966/67, No. 114, fig. 87.

Drost (1933) already realized that this must be Elsheimer's earliest surviving drawing. It is contained in an album 'Klebeband' which can be traced back to the Strasbourg painter Friedrich Brentel (1580–1651), and which Wegner has described and analysed in detail. Some of the little drawings which make up the album are tokens of friendship from other artists, others are copies by Brentel himself. With very few exceptions it can be shown that the drawings originated in Strasbourg, as J. E. von Borries pointed out to me, and this would very likely also apply to the contribution by Elsheimer. It is of significance that the sheet which followed Elsheimer's sketch in the album is a drawing by Johann Vetter Jun., the son of the Frankfurt glass-painter of the same name, with whom Elsheimer collaborated in the design of an armorial window (Cat. 28), dated 1596. Hence von Borries surmised that both artists were in Strasbourg before 1596, possibly to make contact with the famous glass-painting studio of Lingg. Decidedly upper-Rhenish stylistic characteristics (Tobias Stimmer and Christoph Murer) can be detected in the window design, so that a sojourn of the two young artists in Strasbourg seems indeed highly probable. The *Fama* drawing, however, is also very much in the tradition of Jost Amman's woodcuts (for example the *Signeten* which he made for the Frankfurt publisher Feyerabend).

The sentiment of the quatrain is the same as that reflected in Goltzius's drawings of 1600 (Albertina and The Hague: Reznicek, K 195/6, pls. 354/5); it declares that honour comes before gold, a precept echoed by Rembrandt's entry in an autograph book that 'an upright soul respects honour before wealth' (quoted from Chr. White, *Rembrandt as an Etcher*, London 1969, p. 4), reflecting the social qualities expected from an artist or from a 'virtuoso'.

28. Design for an Armor
Düsseldorf, Kunstmuseum (
Pen and wash, 313×203.
Elsheimer and Johannes
Ehlsheimer und Johannes Ve
Kattarina Sein Ehliche Hauss

PROVENANCE: Collection

LITERATURE: Drost 1933,
1957, p. 112; Möhle 1966,

EXHIBITION: Frankfurt 196

The two signatures are au
collaborated in this design
the Frankfurt butcher Phili
Katharina, who in 1579 h
Elsheimer's sisters. The l
portraits and crests of the
shows, as J. E. von Borrie
from designs for glass-p
quotes in particular (fron
by Niklaus von Riedt (In
XI 14 and 15). This wo
quoted in Cat. 27—that V
in Strasbourg before the
upper part, by the eigh
battle with Turks, obviou
the Imperial army in the
earlier. This is a vivid, ev
apprentice, though the a
tionen (Cat. 55) and the '
(Cat. 27, 30, 32) is rea
figure of the dead sol
prostrate Saul in the Fra
may have supplied, as s
scene (cf. drawing of
U.15.25/26).

29. The King of Bali
Copenhagen, Statens M
Pen and grey wash,
numbered *No. 8* below
AE in ink.

PROVENANCE: Unknov

LITERATURE: K. And
Houtman's Journey to
XIII, No. 1, 1975, p. 3.

This is the only prelim
for the etchings that ac
journey (Pls. 7, 10, 11
tionen for 1598. This co
surmised, that Elsheim
plates—the fourth, a *V*
of Georg Keller, also a
op. cit., p. 7). It is th
directly connected wi

composition, as well as that of all the other prints, is clearly based on the engravings (Pl. 9) which illustrated the two first accounts of Houtman's journey: *Verhael van de reyse naer O. Indien*, Middelburgh 1597, and (Willem Lodewycksz.) *D'Eerste boek. Historie van Indien . . .*, Amsterdam (Corn. Claesz.), 1598.

30. A Painter presented to Mercury (Plate 24)

Braunschweig, Herzog-Anton-Ulrich Museum (Inv. 070). Pen and wash, 87×143. Inscribed: *Adamus Ehlsheimer von Franckfurtt 98*. Verso: a dead hare, inscribed: *Stöffen wösteiner Maller zu Müneh(en) gescheh(en) zu Salzpurg 1595*.

PROVENANCE: Unknown.

LITERATURE: Weizsäcker, 'Elsheimers Lehr- und Wanderzeit in Deutschland', in *Jahrbuch der Königlich-Preussischen Kunstsammlungen*, XXXI, 1910, p. 177; Drost 1933, pp. 73, 119, fig. 59; W I, pp. 31, 56 (n. 79); Bothe, pp. 36, 64, pl. 9; W II, p. 158; Drost 1957, p. 107; Möhle 1966, No. 3, pl. 3; vG-J II, p. 28; Hohl 1973, pp. 178, 200 (n. 30).

EXHIBITIONS: *Deutsche Maler und Zeichner des 17. Jahrhunderts*, Berlin 1966, No. 119; Frankfurt 1966/67, No. 115, fig. 88; *Deutsche Kunst des Barock*, Braunschweig 1975, No. 62 (catalogue entry by Chr. von Heusinger).

Like the *Fama* drawing (Cat. 27), this is also part of an 'album amicorum', which has been taken apart. However, most of the sheets, which are also in the Braunschweig Print Room and which can be reassembled because of size and type of paper, point to an owner of the album who lived in or around Munich (cf. verso of the Elsheimer drawing) and are mainly dated between 1595 and 1598 (see Braunschweig Cat., p. 47). As both the signature and the date are undoubtedly in Elsheimer's own hand, this would suggest that his contribution was made during the time he spent in the Munich region, en route from Frankfurt to Venice.

The iconography of the drawing has in the past been wrongly interpreted, and this author too has been misrepresented by Hohl—no doubt through a misunderstanding. A young painter—probably intended as an implied self-portrait—is being presented, perhaps by a Muse, to Mercury the patron and genius of the visual arts, as he was known from Cartari's *Imagini delli Dei* (1556 ff.) *Mercurio inventore . . . delle buone arti*, and as Goltzius was also to depict him in 1611 in the painting at Haarlem (Frans Hals Museum, Inv. 471). Heusinger (Braunschweig Cat. 1975) refers to similar emblemata by Alciati (1551) and Nikolaus Reusner (1581). vG-J II, p. 28, pointed out that Mercury was also the patron of travellers.

The painting leaning on the right, to which the putto points, does not represent 'The Flaying of Marsyas', as Weizsäcker and many later critics have maintained, nor, as Hohl says, the story of Deidameia. Drost correctly saw not a bound male but a female figure. This can be identified as 'Poverty', with wings on one hand (C. Ripa, *Iconologia*, ed. 1764-6, IV, p. 394: *Povertà in uno che abbia bell'ingegno*). The Satyr who pulls her down stands for wordly, everyday things (Ripa, op. cit., IV, p. 155), so that the whole image could be said to represent 'Genius aspiring to virtue being weighed down by common worries and poverty'. This

allegory in connection with the art of painting seems to have been a favourite subject at this period: there is an early drawing by Rottenhammer (Pl. 114), signed and dated 1587, at Düsseldorf (Inv. FP 5636r), and an album-drawing, very similar in conception to Elsheimer's, by Gabriel Weyer (Pl. 117), signed and dated 1616 (Berlin, Inv. KDZ 7645).

31. A Judgement Scene (Plate 34)

Amsterdam, Rijksmuseum, Rijksprentenkabinet (Inv. 15384). Pen and ink, 184×120. Irregularly torn along left-hand margin. On the verso: *helshamer*.

PROVENANCE: Henri Guérard (1846–94), Paris. Acquired 1972.

LITERATURE: K. G. Boon, 'Een compositie-schets van Adam Elsheimer', in *Bulletin van het Rijksmuseum*, XX, 2, 1972, p. 88, fig. 1; Hohl 1973, p. 193, fig. 5.

Boon recognized the stylistic connection between this recently discovered drawing and the larger of the two sheets with figures studies in Berlin (Cat. 34). In fact the nude figure on the left of the raised podium in the Amsterdam drawing seems almost the same as the monk-like figure in the Berlin sheet, whilst the youth with the candle has affinities with the nude figure seen from the rear again on the Berlin sheet. This might lead one to suspect that there are more than accidental connections between the two drawings. The Berlin sheet has the curious inscription DOMITIAN/ANNO and might possibly give the clue to the subject matter of the Amsterdam sheet. Could it be an incident from the story of the Roman Emperor Domitian (81–96), during whose reign of terror people were put to death, the execution of the descendants of David was ordered and St. John banished (Eusebius, *The Ecclesiastical History*, transl. K. Lake. Loeb Classics edition, 1926, I, p. 233)? What is almost certain is that the scene alludes to an episode in the Old or New Testament, as the two attendant figures with turbans signify (Elsheimer used them invariably in biblical subjects), so that Boon's suggestion that what is depicted is the judgement on the sons of Brutus for plotting against the Republic is probably not correct. It is difficult to come to a conclusion, as the composition has been truncated at the left. In fact, it may be asked whether the scene is one of judgement and not rather one of pardon or continence, for the gesture of the standing figure on the left—just risen from his seat and obviously of central importance—appears to be a benevolent one.

Other suggestions for the interpretation of the scene are *David being reconciled to Absalom* (2 Samuel 14) or *The Book of the Covenant read before inhabitants of Jerusalem*, an incident from the Story of Josiah which Heemskerck illustrated in a rather similar composition (Hollstein 241).

The arrangement, with its prominent two tiers, is reminiscent of *Ecce Homo* compositions, such as Rottenhammer's version at Kassel (Pl. 108; also quoted by Boon) and later on favoured by Callot and Rembrandt. But this cannot be the solution to the subject matter of the Amsterdam drawing. It must also be doubted whether the three central figures are supposed to be shown naked, or whether this is not rather a kind of 'shorthand' which the artist employed.

Stylistically there are still echoes from Venetian influences (Palma Giovane) and Rottenhammer.

32. Neptune and Triton (Plate 25)

Dresden, Staatliche Kunstsammlungen, Kupferstichkabinett (Inv. C 2310).

Pen and wash, 104 × 153. Inscribed: *Adam Ehlsheim/in Roma 1600.*

PROVENANCE: Gottfried Wagner (1653–1725), a Leipzig architect and town-councillor, whose widow sold his collection of drawings to Dresden (22 July 1728); in a Dresden inventory of 1738, Cat. 1 mentions 'an Elsheimer drawing'. (This information from Christian Dittrich, Dresden.)

LITERATURE: Bode 1883, pp. 239, 306; Woerman, *Handzeichnungen alter Meister im Kupferstichkabinett zu Dresden*, III, 1896, No. 107, pl. 23; Drost 1933, p. 119, pls. 58 and 70; W I, p. 33, pl. 4; Möhle 1966, No. 4, fig. 3; vG-J II, p. 28.

EXHIBITION: Frankfurt 1966/67, No. 116, fig. 89.

This drawing and Elsheimer's entry in the album of Abel Prasch (Doc. 2) are the first documentary evidence of the artist's arrival in Rome in 1600. Like *Fama* and *Mercury* (Cat. 27 and 30) it is a page from an 'album amicorum', but the advance in technical ability is so evident that, from among all the surviving early drawings, this can be said to reveal for the first time Elsheimer's true individual style and his real potential. All further drawings have been assessed by this sheet. Like the Amsterdam drawing (Cat. 31), the modelling of the figures clearly shows the influences he absorbed in Venice (Palma Giovane and Rottenhammer).

33. The Denial of Peter (Plate 26)

Zürich, Collection Kurt Meissner.

Pen and brown ink, 125 × 168. Laid down. Inscribed on back: *April 1819/from the Wyatt Collection. (Hendrick Goudt—* erased).

PROVENANCE: (The date inscribed on the verso and the reference to the Wyatt Collection do not coincide: there were two sales from the Richard Wyatt collection, at Smith, 19–27 March and at Christie, 19–20 April 1813, but in neither catalogue can this drawing be identified); Victor Bloch, London.

LITERATURE: W. Sumowski, 'Hoogstraten und Elsheimer', in *Kunstchronik*, XIX, 1966, p. 302; Möhle 1966, No. 9a, pl. 8; Hohl 1973, p. 182.

EXHIBITIONS: *Deutsche Maler und Zeichner des 17. Jahrhunderts*, Berlin 1966, No. 123; Frankfurt 1966/67, No. 121, fig. 94; *Old Master Drawings from the collection of Kurt Meissner*, Stanford University (Stanford Art Book 10), 1969, No. 4.

The drawing went under the name of Goudt (whose name was erased from the back of the drawing) until Werner Sumowski recognized it as an original from Elsheimer's hand. It is a good example for comparison with Goudt's style: whereas in the case of Goudt, the apparent freedom of the pen strokes leads so often to impatience and wildness, here the *mise en scène*, the scale of the figures and the bold modelling of both figures and drapery, all speak eloquently for Elsheimer himself. Hence Hohl's assessment that it could only be 'at best by a pupil' is incomprehensible. Stylistically the Meissner drawing is very close to the sheet in Berlin with the seated bearded man (Cat. 37) and the two sheets of figure

studies (Cat. 34 and 35), and i[...] of his creations.

The interpretation of the s[...] not absolutely certain—the [...] with Peter warming himself [...] the forward movement of t[...] towards the figure of Peter, sh[...] That Elsheimer did render [...] the third entry in the 1610 [...] *prospettiva dove doveva essere* [...] *Gesu Christo Nostro Signore* [...] and the 1649 Sale Abraham [...] *een cleyn copere plaert daer* [...] *no. 104* (Denucé, p. 123).

34. Large Sheet of Figur[...]

Berlin-Dahlem, Staatliche [...] (Inv. KDZ 4636).

Pen and brown ink, 265 [...] margin: MEA/DOMITIAN A[...] later hand and covered by [...] (Probably cut along the [...] corner repaired.) Waterm[...] circle (Ferrara 1599)—see [...]

PROVENANCE: August G[...] 1913.

LITERATURE: E. Bock, [...] *Alter Meister im Kupfersti*[...] etc. Berlin 1921, p. 160[...] pl. 58; Drost 1957, pp. [...] 1966, No. 5, pl. 4.

EXHIBITIONS: *Deutsche* [...] Berlin 1966, No. 120; F[...]

This sheet of unconnect[...] of the earliest drawing[...] now largely illegible la[...] as to the exact date. It se[...] most if not all the figu[...] of older or contempo[...] Rome. (His comparison[...] that in a drawing by [...] vincing, as the two fig[...] on this sheet are specif[...] heads in various poses, [...] of a standing youth w[...] ness. These studies of [...] rear seem closely co[...] Amsterdam drawing [...]

35. Small Sheet of [...]

1602–3 (Plate 37)

Berlin-Dahlem, Staat[...] KDZ 5024).

Pen and brown ink, [...] well as along the lo[...] *? Amis suo.* On the v[...] (not in Italian, as M[...]

PROVENANCE: A. v[...]

LITERATURE: Bode 1883, p. 305; E. Bock, *Staatliche Museen. Die Zeichnungen Alter Meister im Kupferstichkabinett. 1: Die deutschen Meister*, etc., Berlin 1921, p. 160, pl. 153; Drost 1933, p. 128; W I, pp. 127, 284; Drost 1957, p. 102; Möhle 1966, No. 6, pl. 5.

EXHIBITIONS: *Aufgang der Neuzeit*, Nuremberg 1952, No. R29; *Deutsche Maler und Zeichner des 17. Jahrhunderts*, Berlin 1966, No. 121; Frankfurt 1966/67, No. 118, fig. 92.

Stylistically this sheet is closely allied to the other two studies of heads and figures, also at Berlin (Cat. 34 and 37). The bearded man with open mouth is almost an elaboration of the head in the lower right corner of the Large Sheet at Berlin, while the semi-nude man with the whip—reminiscent of Domenichino's flagellant in the fresco in the Oratorio di S. Andrea (S. Gregorio al Celio)—seems close to the nude figure in the larger sheet. The figure of the older man with the fur-cap is a typical Elsheimer type and occurs in the Edinburgh *St. Stephen* (Cat. 15) as well as in the background of the Amsterdam drawing (Cat. 31).

> Text of letter on verso:
> *Freundlicher lieber Sr. Nicola so ihr noch frisch und gesundt seid wehre es mir eine sunderliche Freude zu hoeren & es ist mein freundliche bit und begehren an ... wel ... diesen beigelegten briff auff das allerfreundlichst einer Spanisch cortisana zustellen welche genannt wirdt wie ihr auf dem beigelegten briff ...*
>
> (Kind and dear Sr. Nicola, it would give me great pleasure to hear that you are still fresh and in good health and it is my friendly request and desire ... to deliver the enclosed letter very kindly to a Spanish courtesan, whose name is as on the enclosed letter ...).

36. Pietà. About 1601–2 (Plate 41)

Weimar, Kunstsammlungen, Schlossmuseum (Inv. KK 482).
Pen and brown ink, 69 × 55.

PROVENANCE: Unknown.

LITERATURE: Möhle 1966, No. 10, pl. 12.

The drawing was first published by Möhle, who also recognized its relationship to the *Pietà* painting (Cat. 14) which he, however, did not accept as an original by Elsheimer. Möhle also recognized the stylistic affinities between the Weimar drawing and the two Berlin sheets with figure studies. Whether the drawing can be said to be a preparatory study for the painting is not certain, for there are differences: the tiny architectural and landscape details, as well as the lower part of the cross, with a ladder leaning against it, are omitted in the painting, but the relation between the two figures and their poses are so close that it is reasonable to admit the connection.

37. A Seated Bearded Man; in the Background Horsemen and Fleeing Figures. About 1601–2 (Plate 39)

Berlin-Dahlem, Staatliche Museen, Kupferstichkabinett (Inv. KDZ 5087).
Pen and brown ink, 86 × 140. (Whole sheet 90 × 142.) Cut all round and repaired along upper margin; a hole in the centre of the bearded man repaired and restored.

PROVENANCE: A. von Beckerath; acquired 1902.

LITERATURE: Bode 1883, p. 305; Bode 1920, fig. 33; E. Bock, *Staatliche Museen. Die Zeichnungen Alter Meister im Kupferstichkabinett. 1: Die deutschen Meister*, etc., Berlin 1921, p. 159, pl. 149; Drost 1957, p. 101, fig. 126; Möhle 1966, No. 9, pl. 8; Hohl 1973, p. 201, n. 43.

EXHIBITIONS: *Aufgang der Neuzeit*, Nuremberg 1952, No. R30; *Deutsche Maler und Zeichner des 17. Jahrhunderts*, Berlin 1966, No. 122; Frankfurt 1966/67, No. 120, fig. 95.

It has always been assumed that foreground and background of this drawing belong together, but it may well be that—as on the other sheets with figure studies—these are two disconnected exercises. It is not clear whom the man in the front is supposed to represent: Bode suggested Judas (moneybag on the right), others a butcher (holding a knife). The significance of the background scene too has not been clarified: *The Taking of Christ* has been considered, but it seems more likely that it represents a group of prisoners or fleeing people.

Stylistically, the drawing is perfectly consistent with the other Berlin sheets of Studies (Cat. 34 and 35) and the Amsterdam drawing (Cat. 31) and Hohl's suggestion that it could be by either of the Pynas brothers seems therefore misconceived.

38. Angels ministering to Christ. About 1603–5 (Plate 45)

Frankfurt, Städelsches Kunstinstitut (Inv. 15205).
Pen and brown wash, 87 × 197.

PROVENANCE: Count Pocci; Baron Pržibram; R. A. Peltzer; acquired 1927.

LITERATURE: Drost 1933, p. 125, fig. 65; W I, p. 167, fig. 86; W II, pp. 22, 141, 217; Drost 1957, p. 112, fig. 134; Möhle 1966, p. 127, No. 20.

EXHIBITION: Frankfurt 1966/67, No. 128, fig. 98.

The incident depicted comes from Matthew 4:11 and Mark 1:13 and shows Christ being served by Angels after His temptation by the Devil (seen in the drawing at the very top). It is not as great an iconographical rarity as previous writers have led one to believe: Pigler (*Barockthemen* I, p. 271) lists several works—earlier than or contemporary with Elsheimer—mainly by Bolognese painters: Ludovico Carracci, Albani (Grenoble) and Lanfranco (Naples), as well as by the Flemish artists Jan Soens and Frans Francken II. Hence the very generalized description of the painting in the Villa Borghese (Domenico Montelatici, *Villa Borghese*, 1700, p. 226) to which Weizsäcker first drew attention in connection with Elsheimer's composition, may well refer to a picture by another artist. However, a painting of the subject attributed to Elsheimer, but without giving any further description, was included in the sale of pictures from the collection Motteux. It was No. 75 in a Sale of which only an undated and unpriced manuscript catalogue survives in the Victoria and Albert Museum Library (Reserve. S. 1 and 2; a photocopy of the bundle of manuscript-catalogues, of which the Motteux forms part, is also in the Bibliothèque Nationale, Paris: YD 4254 4to). Frank Simpson ('Dutch Paintings in England before 1760', in *Burlington Magazine*, 1953, p. 40, n. 6) believes that the manuscript was compiled by Richard Houlditch (father and son). Peter Anthony Motteux (1660–1718) was a dramatist, librettist and translator (Don Quixote), but was also a dealer in pictures. Pictures from his collection appear in Sales between 1711 and 1759, so that it is likely that the painting entitled *Angels ministering to Jesus—Elsheimer* appeared also on the London market within this span. It may well have been the same painting which featured in the Sale, Jan van Beuningen, Amsterdam, 13 May 1716, Lot 84: 'Christus in de Woestyne bespyst, door Elshamer. 28–0.' It has not been traced and it must thus remain conjectural whether Hollar made his etching of 1652 from the painting which later came into Motteux's possession, or from the drawing.

Weizsäcker's doubts about the originality of this drawing are not justified: the rendering of the figures is typical for Elsheimer and the forms of the trees very close to those in the Berlin landscape (Cat. 42). The sheet appears to have been cut along the left vertical margin and possibly on the right as well, to judge by Hollar's etching. It was folded three times at one time.

ETCHING: Hollar 1652. With the inscription *AElsheimer inv:* (Parthey 99).

DRAWING: Possibly connected—Sale, Amsterdam, Tolling, 21 November 1768, B.nr.122 *Christus verzogt van den Satan in de Woestyne, met de pen gearccert, door A. Elsheymer,* fl. 4.10, bt. Oets.

COPIES: (a) Düsseldorf, Kunstmuseum (Inv. FP 5079). Pen and wash.

(b) Göttingen, University Collection (Inv. 16.26). Pen and wash.

39. Group of Angels on Clouds (Plate 44)
Berlin-Dahlem, Staatliche Museen, Kupferstichkabinett (Inv. KDZ 3794).
Pen and wash, 109×201. Cut out and laid down.

PROVENANCE: Unknown.

LITERATURE: Bode 1883, p. 305 (wrongly stating that the drawing is inscribed with Elsheimer's name); E. Bock, *Staatliche Museen zu Berlin. Die Zeichnungen Alter Meister im Kupferstichkabinett, I: Die deutschen Meister,* etc. 1921, p. 159; W II, p. 40; Drost 1957, p. 107; Möhle 1966, No. 13, pl. 11.

EXHIBITIONS: *Aufgang der Neuzeit,* Nuremberg 1952, No. R21; Frankfurt 1966/67, No. 124, fig. 90.

It would seem that this fragment, wilfully cut about, presents the top section of an Ascension or Coronation of the Virgin. Drost's rejection of the drawing (in 1957) as being too 'pleasant and pretty' is incomprehensible. It fits perfectly with the drawing of *Angels ministering to Christ* (Cat. 38) and the British Museum female figures and Satyrs (Cat. 40): the facial features, the modelling of the bodies and draperies, the typical pentimenti, all speak for Elsheimer's authorship.

40. Studies of Figures, including Satyrs and a 'Carità' Group. 1602–3 (Plate 38)
London, British Museum (Inv. 5224–70).
Pen and wash, 97×180. Lower left corner repaired. Damp has affected the right side of the paper.

PROVENANCE: Sir Hans Sloane.

LITERATURE: Drost 1957, p. 125; Möhle 1966, No. 12, pl. 10; Hohl 1973, p. 188.

Drost called this drawing 'ra
while Hohl believes it to be
It is difficult to agree with ei
Möhle also believed—a pe
Elsheimer himself. The fea
modelling of bodies and dra
and arabesque-like' as Hohl
with Elsheimer's manner. V
contours which may possibly
Möhle's idea that the whole
from the Italian High Rena
seems incorrect. The relief-
well give such an impression
together: the Caritas group
sculpture (see the Venetian
in the Victoria and Albert M
but it stands in no meaningf
ing it, and Hohl's idea that,
this is a scene from Ovid
disturb the Marriage Feast
Deidameia!) is certainly w

41. The Digging for the
Hamburg, Collection Dr.
Pen, brush and wash, 156×
Inscribed: *AElsheimer inv.*

PROVENANCE: (Most of t
II, p. 32, nn. 52–6) Valeriu
stein (according to Weiz
Catalogue of July 1833)
R. W. P. de Vries, Ams
Sale, R. W. P. de Vries,
but ill.); A. Welcker, An
by descent Mrs. Agnes H

LITERATURE: W II, No.
Document on the Frame
in *Burlington Magazine,*
1966, No. B2; vG-J II,
Möhle's catalogue, in
1968, 95; I. Kennedy, '
Frankfurt Tabernacle',
1971, p. 92.

EXHIBITION: Frankfurt

Weizsäcker realized that
himself—was connected
altar with *The Finding a*
as described in the do
Möhle accepted the dra
it to be a copy, possib
Crinò who first suggest
Professor and Mrs. van
it must be a 'cartoon' w
the copper-panel Alth
that there were 'carto
Rembrandt traced dra
Saenredam made car
many of which sur
vindicated, now that th
as the outlines of the d

It is thus a valuable guide for Elsheimer's drawing style, though the indentations give the whole a rather hard look.

An influence of the composition can be noticed in Moeyaert's etching *Jacob hiding the idols* (v.d. Kellen, 15).

42. Mountainous Landscape. 1602–3 (Plate 40)

Berlin-Dahlem, Staatliche Museen, Kupferstichkabinett (Inv. KDZ 2237).

Pen and brown ink, 176×265. Repairs in lower margin. Folds in the paper smoothed out. Watermark: Briquet 12212: Bird within a circle. Ferrara 1599 (see also Cat. 34).

PROVENANCE: Acquired 1881.

LITERATURE: Bode 1883, p. 305; E. Bock, *Staatliche Museen. Die Zeichnungen Alter Meister im Kupferstichkabinett*. I: *Die deutschen Meister*. etc., Berlin 1921, p. 160, pl. 151; Drost 1933, p. 128; W I, p. 248, pl. 139; M. Eger, *Der Stil der Handzeichnungen des Hendrick Goudt* (Diss.) Erlangen 1952, p. 81; Drost 1957, p. 101; Möhle 1966, No. 21, pl. 14; Hohl 1973, p. 201, n. 43.

EXHIBITIONS: *Aufgang der Neuzeit*, Nuremberg 1952, No. R16; *Deutsche Maler und Zeichner des 17. Jahrhunderts*, Berlin 1966, No. 126; Frankfurt 1966/67, No. 129, fig. 125.

This, in broad outline, is a study for the *Aurora* painting (Cat. 18). Whether it was intended as a preliminary design for the picture, or whether the obviously later painting was fortuitously based on it, cannot be said with certainty. The penwork is not unlike that of the Amsterdam drawing (Cat. 31) and the Berlin sheets with figure studies (Cat. 34 and 35), so that it is reasonable to suggest a date contemporary with them. This would be supported by the watermark on the paper, which is the same as that of the large sheet with sketches (Cat. 34).

Drost's suggestion (1957) that the more strongly articulated figures on the left and the mules were drawn in by another hand, is not convincing—everything appears to be by one and the same hand, and there is nothing that cannot be reconciled with Elsheimer's own style. In fact, it is a key drawing for a comparison with Goudt's drawings, and as such it has been singled out for discussion by Manfred Eger in his (unpublished) dissertation on Goudt's drawing style. Everything Elsheimer does has form, structure and clear arrangement, however free the flow of the pen; Goudt's desire to imitate the immediacy of jotting down an idea or impression becomes impatient, formless and muddly—as many landscape drawings from the Frankfurt 'Klebeband' will quickly show. How Hohl can believe that the Berlin drawing can be by the pedantic Johann König is puzzling.

43. Il Contento (I). About 1607 (Plate 68)

Paris, Musée du Louvre, Cabinet des Dessins (Inv. 33.953). Pen, brown ink, grey wash over black chalk (laid down), 239×330. There appear to be some sketches on the back. Folded double-sheet. Watermark: Heywood 3024. Letter M with star. Rome 1570.

PROVENANCE: Unknown. Formerly as 'Anonymous French, 17th century'.

LITERATURE: K. Andrews, *Adam Elsheimer: Il Contento*, Edinburgh 1971, p. 7, fig. 3.

This is an early, if not the first preliminary idea for the foreground of *Il Contento* (Cat. 19). The main accents, as they appear in the final painting, are already present: Jupiter, carried by his eagle, on high; the upward floating figures of Mercury and Contento; the energetic pulling at the cloak; the sacrificial animals. The background architecture has been boldly, but very summarily, indicated by brush strokes. However, at this stage the whole composition was envisaged strictly along the diagonal and on the central axis, whereas in the two later drawings and in the painting itself the main event has been moved towards the left, allowing the space on the right to be filled by a surging crowd. The major difference between this drawing and the painting is in the right hand side of the composition. It would appear that Elsheimer, in the early stage, intended to represent the self-indulgence and sybaritic way of the people as part of the foreground, a passage which was later to be relegated to the background of the composition. The embracing couple on the extreme right seems like an echo of two figures in Agostino Carracci's engraving *Il reciproco amore* (B.119).

44. Il Contento (II). About 1607 (Plate 69)

Edinburgh, National Gallery of Scotland (Inv. RSA 298). Pen and grey wash over black chalk, 288×374. Two sheets joined together. Contours incised. Watermark: Heywood 1347. Figure bearing a cross. Rome 1570.

PROVENANCE: P. Mariette; David Laing; Royal Scottish Academy; transferred on loan 1966.

LITERATURE: K. Andrews, *Adam Elsheimer: Il Contento*, Edinburgh 1971, p. 9, fig. 4; Hohl 1973, p. 188, fig. 7.

EXHIBITION: *Old Master Drawings from the David Laing Bequest*, Edinburgh 1976, No. 25.

Of the three surviving drawings for *Il Contento*, this appears to be an intermediary state. The temple architecture has been moved to the left so that the two main figures are now in dead centre. The four figures in the foreground of the previous drawing (Cat. 43) have been removed and additional 'crowd' figures substituted. The figures behind the bull have been retained, but they have been more fully worked out, while those of the extreme left have been shifted towards the centre, and the drapery and headgear of the girl with the outstretched arm have been elaborated. The figure of Jupiter, showing various pentimenti, has been tilted forward. The background has again been very broadly indicated with the brush, in a kind of shorthand, by which means also some of the figures in the middle-distance have been suggested, and the tip of the brush has been used very delicately to model the figures (see the back of the nude on the right) and the draperies.

The contours have been incised—also visible in the third surviving drawing (Cat. 45)—which indicates that some of the main figures have been traced through onto another sheet, in order to vary the composition without having to redraw all the figures each time.

COPIES: (a) Leningrad, Hermitage (Inv. 7423, Coll. Cobenzl). Drawing, pen and wash, obviously traced from the Edinburgh drawing.

(b) Vienna, Albertina. (Albertina Cat. IV/V; Deutsche Schulen, No. 521).

45. Il Contento (III). About 1607 (Plate 70)
Paris, Musée du Louvre, Cabinet des Dessins (Inv. 18.657).
Pen and grey wash, 264×417. All contours incised.

PROVENANCE: Unknown.

LITERATURE: L. Demonts, *École du Nord*, II, 1938, No. 558, pl. CXLV, as 'École, ou manière d'Adam Elsheimer'; K. Andrews, *Adam Elsheimer: Il Contento*, Edinburgh 1971, p. 11, fig. 5; Hohl 1973, p. 201, n. 46.

This drawing—nearest to the final painting—looks at first sight the strangest, because it appears to be the most summary, and was therefore dismissed by many as a copy; the latest of these denigrators is Hohl. However, when it is realized that all the figures have very likely been traced onto the sheet from previous drawings and that the present design was achieved chiefly by the stylus—with pen and grey wash rapidly laid in—very much in the manner in which Poussin was to indicate the disposition of light and shade in an elaborate composition a generation or so later, the status of this drawing as an original ought to become clear.

46. Jupiter and Mercury with Philemon (Plate 35)
Berlin-Dahlem, Staatliche Museen, Kupferstichkabinett (Inv. KDZ 5642).
Pen and brown ink, 59×51. Cut all round.

PROVENANCE: A. von Beckerath; acquired 1902.

LITERATURE: E. Bock, *Staatliche Museen zu Berlin. Die Zeichnungen Alter Meister im Kupferstichkabinett*, I: *Die deutschen Meister*, etc., 1921, p. 159, pl. 153; Drost 1933, p. 95; Drost 1957, p. 102, fig. 128; Möhle 1966, No. 11, pl. 12.

EXHIBITIONS: *Aufgang der Neuzeit*, Nuremberg 1952, No. R36; Frankfurt 1966/67, No. 122, fig. 97.

Possibly connected (a first idea?) with the Dresden painting (Cat. 24). One has to imagine the figure of Baucis on the left, behind Philemon, where the paper has been cut. Stylistically the drawing goes well with the Berlin sheets of sketches and the Amsterdam drawing and may thus be dated fairly early in Elsheimer's Roman years, much earlier than the Dresden painting. Amusing, and typical for Elsheimer's interpretation of a story, is the highly informal pose of Mercury.

47. Tobias and the Angel (Plate 73)
Berlin-Dahlem, Staatliche Museen, Kupferstichkabinett (Inv. KDZ 8498).
Gouache, 70×95.

PROVENANCE: Earl Spencer; G. Hibbert; W. Esdaile; N. F. Haym; R. Ph. Goldschmidt; acquired 1917.

LITERATURE: Sale, Prestel, Frankfurt, 4–5 October 1917, No. 191, fig. 76; Drost 1933, p. 140; W I, pp. 125, 295, fig. 67; W II, p. 131; Drost 1957, p. 106 (as anon.).

EXHIBITIONS: *Aufgang der Neuzeit*, Nuremberg 1952, No. R39; *Deutsche Maler und Zeichner des 17. Jahrhunderts*, Berlin 1966, No. 132; Frankfurt 1966/67, No. 144, fig. 108.

Another variant on the Tobias theme, which preoccupied Elsheimer during his Roman years. As Drost and Möhle have said, the composition, the scale of the figures and their relation to the background are akin to the etching (Cat. 58), which has probably been adapted from it, and both, though

in a somewhat remote wa
Small Tobias, in which the
and does not trail it behind

The technique, with the
those gouaches which ca
Elsheimer.

48. Salome receiving the
Chatsworth, Trustees of t
851C).
Gouache, 78×67.

PROVENANCE: N. A. Flinc
Devonshire, 1723.

LITERATURE: Bode 1883,
1925, No. 17; W I, pp. 19c
pl. 27.

EXHIBITIONS: *German A*
No. 172; Frankfurt 1966/

As Möhle pointed out, this
the Inventory of the Rotte
Jakob Loys (1680): *Een*
Elshamer (No. 22 in Brec
p. 1589, and under No. 23
drawing may have been
painting which is now lc
pattern for Goudt's engra
extent from the Chatswc
figures instead of five; wh
sword in Goudt's print, h
drawing, which also lack
boyant feather-cap; and
in the drawing than in (
composed the scene into
copyists have taken o
Chatsworth gouache is
(Hamburg and Zürich, C

COPIES: Two paintings
known: one on copper,
easel in Adam Oeser's *A*
—a picture, literally, wi
hagen (Statens Museum
shape of Elsheimer's dra
(a) Anon. seventeenth ce
for Kunst (Inv. 559). Cc
(b) Anon. seventeenth
in his *Studio* (Pl. 125). I
Kunstsammlungen (Inv
same sense as Goudt's e

ENGRAVINGS: (a) Hendr
Hollstein 4. (Pl. 94)
(b) W. Hollar, 1646. Et
(c) R. V. Forst. Copy a
(d) Anon. Mezzotint.
Possibly by either John
Vaillant.

49. The Bath of Batt
Vienna, Albertina (Inv.
Gouache, 91×84.

PROVENANCE: ? Johann Thomas Richter (1728–73), Leipzig (as Möhle has stated, the drawing may have belonged to Richter—a Leipzig merchant and collector—as he is depicted with it in a portrait by Anton Graff (c. 1700), engraved by Bause in 1775).

LITERATURE: Bode 1883, p. 304; Albertina Catalogue IV/V: *Zeichnungen der deutschen Schulen*, No. 513, pl. 163; Möhle 1966, No. 36, pl. 23.

The free handling of the brush and the almost 'impressionistic' indication of the landscape background (like that in the *Il Contento* drawings, Pls. 68–70), and the superb modelling of the attendant woman, all point to an original Elsheimer drawing. The version in Berlin (Möhle 35), which has always been accepted as an original and even on occasion as superior to the Vienna drawing, has all the appearance of a copy: the figures are flat and wooden and the drapery without volume, while the trees and bushes, though apparently more detailed, are lifeless and superficial. Typical for Elsheimer's faithfulness to the essentials of the narrative is the rapidly sketched-in figure of David on the tower, in the top of the Vienna drawing, missing in the Berlin version. The Bathsheba in the Berlin drawing may well have been derived from, or perhaps influenced, the Venus in the large gouache with *Venus and Amor*, formerly in the Koenigs collection, but now lost, which belongs to the group—possibly by Battem—comprising the Louvre, Berlin, London, Edinburgh and Dublin drawings (Möhle 46–8, 57 and 64).

50. The Mocking of Ceres (Plate 83)
Hamburg, Kunsthalle (Inv. 1927–105).
Gouache, 159×104.

PROVENANCE: ? Guichardot, according to an inscription on the back, but not apparently in the Sale, Paris, 7–20 July 1875; E. Calando; Sale, Paris, Druout, 7–18 March 1927, Lot 114; F. Lugt; acquired 1927.

LITERATURE: W I, pp. 189, 263, pl. 93; W II, p. 42; Drost 1957, pp. 58, 115, fig. 67; Möhle 1966, No. 37, fig. 25.

EXHIBITIONS: *Deutsche Maler und Zeichner des 17. Jahrhunderts*,

Berlin 1966, No. 131; Frankfurt 1966/67, No. 140, fig. 105. Elsheimer was obviously greatly preoccupied with the story of Ceres and her search for her daughter Proserpina, during which she encountered the old woman and the mocking boy, whom she changes into a lizard (Ovid, v, 446). The best known result is the composition as we know it from the painting in the Prado, which depicts the same incident as the present drawing, whereas a later aspect of the story is represented in the drawing in the Meissner collection (Cat. 51).

51. Ceres changing the Mocking Boy into a Lizard (Plate 84)
Zürich, Collection Kurt Meissner.
Gouache, 110×68. Inscribed on the back, in a nineteenth-century hand: 'A. Elsheimer f geb. Frankfurt 1574'.

PROVENANCE: J. A. G. Weigel, Leipzig (1836); Sale, Gutekunst, Stuttgart, 15 May 1883, Lot 285; Sale, Stephen List, Frankfurt, 10–11 October 1969, Lot 120, as 'Elsheimer Workshop'.

LITERATURE: K. Andrews, 'A rediscovered Elsheimer Drawing', in *Master Drawings*, IX, 1, 1971, p. 38, pl. 16.

The various slight disfigurations (oxydization and 'strengthening' by another hand) in certain passages led to the description of the drawing in the 1969 sale as a workshop product. However, compared with the other gouaches that can be attributed to Elsheimer, this seems a perfectly genuine work. The modelling of the face and neck of the old woman and the way the light plays around the figures—which no copyist could imitate—all speak for a genuine drawing. The nearest parallels are the Hamburg *Ceres* drawing (Cat. 50), the little *Tobias* in Berlin (Cat. 47), and the Chatsworth *Salome* (Cat. 48).

The drawing again demonstrates Elsheimer's continued fascination with the Ceres theme. The beginning of Ovid's story can be seen in the Hamburg drawing and the Prado version of the painting, whereas the present work (never, as far as it is known, translated into a painting) shows the end of the episode, when the boy, having mocked the thirsty goddess, has been changed by her into a lizard (Ovid, v, 446–61).

PRINTS

52. Adam and Eve. About 1597 (Plate 4)
Brussels, Bibliothèque Royale, Cabinet des Estampes.
Engraving, 203×163.

PROVENANCE: Charles van Hulthem (1764–1832); Sale, van Hulthem, Ghent, 8 June 1846, No. 527.

LITERATURE: J. D. Passavant, *Archiv für Frankfurts Geschichte und Kunst*, 4tes Heft, 1847, p. 74, No. 8; Hind, No. 14; W II, p. 125, No. 1; Hollstein, VI, No. 14.

EXHIBITIONS: L. de Pauw, *Charles van Hulthem*, Brussels 1964, No. 124; Frankfurt 1966/67, No. 258, fig. 164.

This impression is the only one that has survived. The composition has been copied from an engraving by Jan Sadeler after Marten de Vos (Wurzbach 4). Weizsäcker (II, p. 35) drew attention to a stained-glass painting of the same composition (in reverse) in the Historical Museum at Frankfurt,

dated 1594. The Brussels engraving bears no signature, but the tradition—going back to Passavant—that this is an early experiment of print-making by the young Elsheimer is a perfectly acceptable one.

53. Allegory of Fortune. About 1597 (Plate 5)
Etching, 118×95.

LITERATURE: H. Voss, 'Aus der Umgebung Altdorfers und Wolf Hubers', in *Mitteilungen der Gesellschaft für vervielfältigende Kunst (Die Graphischen Künste)*, Vienna 1909, No. 4, p. 76; Hind, p. 28, No. 10; W II, p. 129, No. 14; Hollstein, VI, p. 148, No. 10; Andrews MJ 1973, p. 163, fig. 6.

EXHIBITION: Frankfurt 1966/67, No. 267, fig. 173.

Voss thought the work to be by an anonymous artist under the influence of Altdorfer; Hind thought it could possibly be by Elsheimer; while both Weizsäcker and Hollstein accept it as an original work by Elsheimer. (The impression in the British Museum came in 1836 from the Sheepshanks collection with an attribution to Elsheimer.) It is obviously an abandoned experiment by a person not experienced in the art of etching. The impact of Altdorfer, which Voss recognized, is evident (cf. the female attendant in *Susannah's Bath* in Munich, Pl. 107) as well as a remoter echo from Dürer's *Nemesis* engraving; Elsheimer transformed these models into his own interpretation. Probably from his period of apprenticeship with Uffenbach.

54. Boy with a Horse. About 1597 (Plate 6)
Etching, 197×155.

LITERATURE: Hind, p. 28, No. 6; W I, pl. 167; W II, p. 126, No. 6; Hollstein, VI, p. 145, No. 6; H. Möhle, 'Drawings by Jacques de Gheyn III', in *Master Drawings*, I/2, 1963, p. 7; Andrews MJ 1973, p. 164, fig. 9.

EXHIBITION: Frankfurt 1966/67, No. 263, fig. 174.

Möhle's ascription of this work to de Gheyn the Younger seems misconceived. It is one more example of Elsheimer's intense absorption of Dürer's work: in this case it is the engraving of the *Large Horse*, which also was the prototype of Caravaggio's *Conversion of Saul* (Rome, S. Maria del Popolo), a work to which Weizsäcker, and those that followed him, pointed when searching for an influence on Elsheimer. However, this etching appears to be from Elsheimer's German period: the two dogs are based on Dürer's *St. Eustace* engraving, while the groom is reminiscent once again of one of Elsheimer's earliest and most persistent influences: Jost Amman (*Artliche unnd Kunstreiche Figuren zu der Reutterey*, 1584, fol. Q iv).

55. Illustrations to Houtman's 'Journey to the East Indies'. 1598 (Plates 7, 10, 11)
(a) Map of the two hemispheres with portraits of Columbus and Vespucci. Signed *AE* (in monogram) and dated [15]98.
(b) South African and Malay native types. (Divided into four compartments.)
(c) Native types from Sunda, Sumatra and Java. (Divided into four compartments), the last signed *AE* (in monogram) and dated 1598.
Etchings, 229×300.

LITERATURE: O. Donner von Richter, 'Philip Uffenbach und andere gleichzeitig in Frankfurt a.M. lebende Maler', in *Archiv für Frankfurter Geschichte und Kunst*, VII, 1901; Hind, pp. 26–7, Nos. 2–4; W I, p. 40, pl. 8; W II, p. 128, No. 10; Hollstein, VI, p. 144, No. 21; K. Andrews, 'Elsheimer's Illustrations for Houtman's "Journal to the East Indies" ', in *Master Drawings*, XIII/1, 1975, p. 3.

EXHIBITION: (a): Frankfurt 1966/67, No. 266.

These etchings were appended to the account of Cornelis Houtman's expedition in 1595–7 to the East Indies (the beginning of the Dutch overseas empire), which was published in the Frankfurt *Messrelationen* for 1598. These were news-sheets, issued during the Spring and Autumn fairs at Frankfurt and reporting happenings from all over the world. Uffenbach and his pupils were frequent contributors of illustrations to these *Messrelationen*. Noticing the initials AE

on two of the etchings, Donn[...]
suggest that their author was [...]
whose name fitted the initial[...]
followed this view, which [...]
discovery, in the Copenhag[...]
preliminary drawing for one [...]
been proved that all the co[...]
illustrations contained in tw[...]
journey, published in Mid[...]
spectively the year previous[...]
n. 9). Although the title-pa[...]
globe and the two portrait[...]
route which Houtman took [...]
book by Linschoten of a vo[...]
(Andrews, p. 6), Weizsäcke[...]
its style is derived from the [...]
Tobias Stimmer.

The fourth plate, a *View of* [...]
ing the *Messrelationen*, which [...]
by previous writers, is no[...]
technically different from t[...]
Georg Keller, another of [...]
p. 7).

56. The Mocking of Cer[...]
Hamburg, Kunsthalle (Inv. [...]
Etching, 314×233 (whole [...]
position).

PROVENANCE: W. Esdaile. [...]

LITERATURE: W I, pl. 92; [...]
p. 150, without number.

EXHIBITION: Frankfurt 19[...]

A unique impression, and [...]
drawings and painting o[...]
occupied Elsheimer for s[...]
compare the inferior qual[...]
the superb quality of Gou[...]

57. Joseph and the Chri[...]
Etching, 110×87. Signed [...]

LITERATURE: Hind, p. 26, [...]
No. 4; Hollstein, VI, p. 1[...]

EXHIBITION: Frankfurt 19[...]

The composition is the sa[...]
the little panels at Petwo[...]
predates the painting, or [...]
impossible to say. The [...]
etching needle is typical f[...]
fought with this, for him [...]

58. Tobias and the An[...]
Etching, 92×146.

LITERATURE: Hind, p. 28 [...]
No. 3; Hollstein, VI, p. 1[...]

EXHIBITION: Frankfurt 1 [...]

The composition repeat[...]
the dog in front and the [...]
the *Small Tobias* (Cat. 2[...]

59. **Nymph** Dancing **with Tambourine and Satyrs**
(Plate 96)
Etching, 63× 100.

LITERATURE: Hind 9; W I, pl. 166; W II, p. 127, No. 9;
Hollstein, VI, p. 147, No. 9.

EXHIBITION: Frankfurt 1966/67, No. 265, fig. 167.

Although Hind includes it among the original etchings by
Elsheimer, and Hollar copied it, I am a little uneasy whether
to accept it as an Elsheimer. Like A55 (Hind 12) it could well
be by Willem Basse.

COPY: Hollar (Parthey 279). Etching (in reverse)

REJECTED WORKS

Only the chief works among those that have during recent times persistently been ascrib
with, and wherever possible alternative attributions suggested. To list all works that have
attached to them would fill another book. (References are to the Catalogue of the Fran
literature is quoted.)

PAINTINGS

A1. Myrrha. Frankfurt, Städelsches Kunstinstitut. (Frankfurt 1966/67, No. 30.) By David Teniers I.

A2. The Curse of Latona. London, Coll. Count Seilern. (Frankfurt 1966/67, No. 31.) Waddingham (1972, p. 610, n. 53) believes the painting is by König; I think it may be by one of the Pynas brothers. Attention should, however, be drawn to an etching by Hollar (Parthey 272) of a *Latona* (*AElsheimer pinxit*), then in the Arundel Collection and dated 1640. Of this composition a painted copy exists, in reverse, very close to Poelenburgh, if not actually by him (Coll. Lady Exeter, Burghley House. Courtauld Neg. B57/1524), as well as the *Landscape with a woman and child* (which omits the three male figures), formerly in the Dominion Gallery, Dr. Max Stern at Montreal (W II, pl. 8), which has not been traced. The composition, the figures and the landscape, to judge from Hollar's print, look plausible for Elsheimer, and if the original painting is found, it may well turn out to be an original by him.

A3. Nymph. East Berlin, Staatliche Museen. (Frankfurt 1966/67, No. 34.) Near or by Poelenburgh.

A4. Apollo and Battus. Florence, Uffizi. (Frankfurt 1966/67, No. 40.) E. Schaar has attributed this painting to Breenbergh.

A5. Landscape with the Temple of the Sibyl. Prague, National Gallery. (Frankfurt 1966/67, No. 43.) Various alternative attributions have been suggested: Poelenburgh; Breenbergh (Waddingham); Godfredo Wals (Hohl); Filippo Napoletano (M. Chiarini), with which I agree.

A6. The House on the Hill. Bremen, Kunsthalle. (Frankfurt 1966/67, No. 44.) Although the work of Godfredo Wals is still a matter of speculation, this roundel—like one recently acquired by the Fitzwilliam Museum as Tassi—may be by him.

A7. Hagar in the Desert and **Tobias and the Angel.** Nostell Priory, Lord St. Oswald. (Frankfurt 1966/67, No. 2 and No. 8.) Neither painting is on wood, as stated in the Frankfurt Catalogue, but both are on copper laid on wood.

The birds in the *Hagar* a
paintings appear to be Dut
far as the landscape is conc

A8. Susannah and the
Gallery. (W II, p. 14, N
Waddingham has recent
Thoman von Hagelstein.

A9. The Adoration of
Court. (Waddingham 19
hammer and Bril.

A10. The Rest on th
Stiftung Heylshof. (Fran
Pynas.

A11. The Preaching o
(Frankfurt 1966/67, No.
(Andrews MJ 1973, pl. 1

A12. The Preaching o
Pinakothek. (Frankfurt
Stalbemt (Andrews MJ

A13. The Good Sam
1966/67, No. 15.) By J
with variations, at Nan

A14. Ecce Homo. F
(Frankfurt 1966/67, N
Hagelstein.

A15. The Supper at
(Frankfurt 1966/67, No

A16. The Supper a
(Frankfurt 1966/67, No
near to or by von Hag

A17. The Sacrifice
Kunstinstitut. (Frankfu
Stalbemt (Andrews 19

A18. Hollar. The H
Etching (Parthey 114).
painting has not been

166

the chiefly architectural composition appears unlikely to have been from Elsheimer's hand, unless this was a collaboration between Elsheimer (who designed the figures) and a painter of architectural subjects.

A19. Hollar. **Mercury and Herse.** Etching (Pl. 116; Parthey 268). Inscribed: *AElsheimer pinxit.* An original by Elsheimer seems not to have survived, but on the face of it, the composition, the landscape and the figures could well have been copied from an Elsheimer work, possibly inspired by Virgil Solis's woodcut in the Ovid edition, Frankfurt 1563, p. 33. The group, with some variations, has been incorporated (in reverse) into Jacob Pynas's painting of the same subject (Florence, Galleria Pitti, Inv. 1116; Frankfurt 1966/67,

No. 89, fig. 75) and even there the figures preserve something of an Elsheimer character. A remoter adaptation of the group is contained in the painting by Carlo Antonio Procaccini (1616) in a private collection and published by Longhi in 1965 (*Paragone* 185 Arte, July 1956, p. 53). Another version of the composition, but much nearer to Hollar's etching, is the painting on copper at Chatsworth (Courtauld List No. 356; Neg. no. B75/853), there attributed to 'Bril and Elsheimer'. The landscape, much grander and more elaborate than in the etching, seems certainly to be by Bril. However, I feel that there is no division of hands here, and the whole painting (including the figures) is in fact by Bril himself, to whom it had been attributed till 1725.

DRAWINGS

(The drawings from the so-called Frankfurt 'Klebeband' are not listed again, as I believe them all to be by Goudt. Some of the suggested changes of attributions of the *gouaches* are based on a paper read by the author at the meeting of the Association of Art Historians at Glasgow in March 1976.)

Pen drawings

A20. **Tobias frightened by the fish.** Basle, Private Collection. (Möhle 1966, No. 7.) Like Möhle A9, this seems to me near to or by Jan Pynas.

A21/22. **The Satyr with the peasants.** London, British Museum (Möhle 1966, Nos. 14 and 15). These two drawings appear definitely post-Rembrandt, and I have come independently to the conclusion of Werner Sumowski that they are by G. van den Eeckhout. An attribution to 'Rembrandt School' had already been proposed by Hind (IV, p. 140).

A23. **The Finding of Moses.** Berlin. (Möhle 22.) Hohl's suggestion that this is by Agostino Tassi may well be right.

A24. **Landscape with Tobias and the Angel.** Berlin. (Möhle 23.) This seems to be the same hand as A23, and I cannot see why, if Möhle 22 is by Tassi, this is supposed to be by Filippo Napoletano, as Hohl states.

A25. **Mountain** landscape (*Verso:* Figures). London, British Museum (Möhle 24 and 8). vG-J (II, p. 30) and Hohl have rightly suggested Jan Pynas as the artist of this drawing.

A26. **Landscape with the Mocking of Ceres.** Zürich, Private Collection. (Möhle 25.) This seems the same hand as A23 and A24, hence possibly by Tassi and not by Jan Pynas, as Hohl suggests.

A27. **Landscape with Tobias and the Angel.** Cambridge, Fitzwilliam Museum (Möhle 27). Basically an adaptation of the Large Tobias composition. A27 and A23 were sold together in Lot 82 in the Sale of the Benjamin West collection (Christie's, 13 June 1820) as 'Claude Lorrain' (vG-J II, p. 30, n. 44). I agree with Hohl that both are probably by Tassi.

A28. **Landscape with train of mules.** Berlin. (Möhle 26.) Hohl suggests Jan Pynas. It seems to me to be clearly by Goudt.

A29, 30, 31, 32, 33, 34, 35. **Mountainous landscapes.** Berlin; Frankfurt; Vienna (private coll.); Copenhagen; London (Courtauld Inst.); Frankfurt; formerly private

collection, Amsterdam. (Möhle 26, 28, 29, 30, 31, 32, 33.) All these are by Hendrick Goudt.

A36. **Landscape.** Frankfurt, Städelsches Kunstinstitut. (Möhle 67.) Goudt copying the background of the *Aurora* landscape.

Gouaches

A37. **Venus and Amor.** Formerly Coll. Koenigs. (Möhle 34.)

A38. **Nocturnal riverbank.** Paris, Louvre. (Möhle 46.)

A39. **River landscape with herdsmen.** London, British Museum. (Möhle 48.)

A40. **River landscape with boats.** Berlin. (Möhle 47.)

A41. **Wooded landscape with castle.** Edinburgh, National Gallery of Scotland. (Möhle 57.)

A42. **Wooded landscape with church and house.** Dublin, National Gallery of Ireland. (Möhle 64.)

These six gouaches seem to me by Gerrit van Battem; the Edinburgh drawing (A41) is signed with his name.

A43, 44, 45, 46. **Landscapes.** (Möhle 51 (and verso D19), 52, 53, 60.) These are all likely to be by Pieter de With (and vG-J II, p. 36, deciphered de With's barely legible signature on Möhle 60).

A47. **River landscape with castle.** Mannheim, Coll. Frank. (Möhle 61.) Either by P. de With or Philips Koninck (as H. Gerson proposed in 1936).

A48. **View across a wide landscape.** London, British Museum. (Möhle 62.) Close to Philips de Koninck.

A49. **Mountainous landscape with herdsman.** Basle, Coll. Robert von Hirsch. (Möhle 58.) Copy of the background of Goudt's engraving after the *Large Tobias*.

A50, 51. **Forest fringes.** New York, Pierpont Morgan Library; Frankfurt, Städelsches Kunstinstitut. (Möhle 65, 66 and G43.) By Hendrick Goudt, as the verso of Möhle 66 testifies.

A52. **Hilly landscape.** Leningrad, Hermitage. (Möhle 68.)

Not a gouache, but a drawing with pen and wash. Close to Goudt, if not actually by him.

A53. Landscape with wooded bluff and wanderer. London, Coll. Count Seilern. (Möhle 63.) Not a gouache, but a drawing with pen and wash. The composition is close

to Ruisdael (cf. painting in I̶
gested that the drawing is by
in which the artist has to be
For the other rejected landsc
suggestions to make as to al̶

ETCHINGS

A54. Landscape with the dismissal of Hagar. Inscribed: *AElshaemer f.* (Hind 7.) The background with the Tomb of the Horatii does not seem to be from Elsheimer's hand; the figures appear to have been added.

A55. Resting Satyrs. (Hind 11.)

A56. Satyr piping to two nymphs. (Hind 12.)

A57. **Satyr offering a bu̶**
   As Hind already indicat̶
likely by Willem Basse.

A58. Tobias and the An̶
Berlin drawing (Cat. 47).

APPENDIX : Painting on Copper

Copper as a support for oil painting was known at least as early as the first decade of the sixteenth century, and Vasari reports that Sebastiano del Piombo experimented not only with copper, but also with supports like marble. Karel van Mander in his *Schilderboek* (1604) mentions that Bartholomeus Spranger painted a *Last Judgement* on copper (now in the Turin Gallery) and he lists other northern artists who did likewise, 'according to the method of the Netherlandish artists'. Copper, apart from its use for enamelling, had of course been used for engraving and etching, and it is interesting to note that painting on copper seems to have coincided with a revival of print-making, or an increase in the activity, in Germany and in Venice and Bologna, where copper supports for painting became common. In some instances the copper plate had already been used for engraving before the paint was applied: for example Thoman von Hagelstein's *Judith* (Friedrichshafen) and the so-called Elsheimer *Tobias* (London, National Gallery). The reason for this may have been economy, for compared with more commonly used materials such as wood and canvas, copper was (and still is) rather costly. On the other hand, canvas had on the whole a rather coarser surface and wood panels required rather long and laborious preparation before painting could begin.

At first copper came in the form of large, flat sheets and plates had to be beaten out by hand and cut, so that the production must have been small and costly: for example the copper plates of the Berlin altarpiece with scenes from the *Life of the Virgin* were beaten. Later on in the sixteenth century, rolling mills were invented (some are illustrated in Leonardo's notebooks), which were capable of producing rather smaller sheets of metal more cheaply. The centres of supply of copper were Antwerp (panels with the blind-stamp of the Antwerp coppersmith Pieter Stas are known), Hungary and Tyrol, as well as Amsterdam and Hamburg, whence copper was exported for all kinds of purposes. According to J. G. Krünitz's *Encyklopädie* (Berlin 1794), part XIV, the worst copper was produced in North Italy, so that the artists working in Italy very likely used imported copper plates.

The attraction of painting on copper was no doubt its smooth surface, ideal for fine brushes and delicate detail. The expansion coefficient of copper compares favourably with that of wood. The small size of most copper plates made them suitable for easy transport, so that on occasion two painters could collaborate on one composition, one painting the landscape, the other the figures. Furthermore, copper plates were suitable for letting into pieces of furniture. Generally speaking, painting on copper began in earnest during the second half of the

sixteenth century (Guido Reni copied compositions by Annibale Car
continued well into the seventeenth century, although it was still pop
century. Sebastiano Conca (1680–1764) trained his students in his Ac
Farnese to paint small pictures on copper.

Before being able to paint on copper, the plate must be prepared
have a history of blistering and flaking, and painters in the past proba
important to ensure that there was no corrosion due to chemical in
copper and the oil priming. On the other hand, Joyce Plesters (Nat
has reported that in a painting by Guercino (*Angels weeping over the dea*
Gallery) she discovered 'a green layer of corrosion product that ha
copper panel and the cream-coloured oil priming, presumably as a
action between the copper and the oil and/or resin in the medium
layer had served the useful purpose of bonding the preparation and p
but the presence of such a layer in paintings on copper seems unfortur
rather than the rule.' Old manuals recommended 'roughening' the
garlic, in order to give it a tooth and get the oil paint to adhere to th
Sanderson, *Graphice*, 1658, p. 69). Another method, occasionally u
'silver' the surface of the copper plate before applying a groun
normally a lead–tin alloy, and it is not clear whether it was used i
arrest any harmful reaction between copper and oil or resins, o
experimenting with a lighter surface rather than the brown o
reflection of the 'silver' shine through the superimposed ground a
panels are the exception in his work. There are instances where re
Lorrain, *Coastscene with the embarkation of St. Paul*, Birmingha
there are three paintings by Rembrandt where the white lead pr
was entirely overlaid with gold leaf, which formed the ground for
'Schilderde Rembrandt op goud', in *Oud Holland*, LXXXIV/2–3,
recipes for 'whitening' copper are given in the *Dictionarium Po
Body of Arts Regularly Digested* (London 1735. 2 vols.) and confi
an alloy. On to this 'silvered' surface, often visible along the r
or in places where the paint has chipped off, Elsheimer used
invariably grey in tone, as can be seen in passages where the pair
of the unfinished pictures.

N.B. For further technical details, see the paper read by Dr. J. A. van der Graaf to
International Institute for Conservation of Historic and Artistic Works (IIC), *Conser*
pp. 139 ff.

SELECTED BIBLIOGRAPHY

The literature on Elsheimer is enormous, but most of it is now irrelevant or has been absorbed into the books by Weizsäcker (W I and W II) and Möhle (1966), where full bibliographies can be found. Listed here are the main books and articles to which frequent reference has been made in this book. Others are quoted in the notes and the catalogue entries.

Andrews 1972	Keith Andrews, 'The Elsheimer Inventory and other Documents', in *Burlington Magazine*, September 1972
Andrews 1973	Keith Andrews, 'A Pseudo-Elsheimer Group: Adriaen van Stalbemt as Figure Painter', in *Burlington Magazine*, May 1973
Andrews MJ 1973	Keith Andrews, 'Elsheimer and Dürer: an attempt towards a clarification of Elsheimer's early work', in *Münchner Jahrbuch der bildenden Kunst*. Dritte Folge, XXIV, 1973
Bode 1883	Wilhelm Bode, *Studien zur Geschichte der holländischen Malerei*. 1883
Drost 1933	Willi Drost, *Adam Elsheimer und sein Kreis*. 1933
Drost 1957	Willi Drost, *Adam Elsheimer als Zeichner*. 1957
Frankfurt 1966–67	*Adam Elsheimer: Werk, Künstlerische Herkunft und Nachfolge*. Exhibition at the Städelsches Kunstinstitut Frankfurt. December 1966–January 1967 (Introduction by Ernst Holzinger; Catalogue by Jutta Held)
Hind	A. M. Hind, 'Adam Elsheimer II. His original etchings', in *The Print Collector's Quarterly*, XIII, 1926
Hollstein	F. W. Hollstein, *Dutch and Flemish Etchings, Engravings and Woodcuts*. Amsterdam 1954 etc.
Holzinger 1951	Ernst Holzinger, 'Elsheimers Realismus', in *Münchner Jahrbuch der bildenden Kunst*, II, 1951
Möhle 1966	Hans Möhle, *Die Zeichnungen Adam Elsheimers*. 1966
Sandrart	Joachim von Sandrart, *Teutsche Akademie*, etc. (1675), ed. A. R. Peltzer. 1925
vG-J I	J. G. van Gelder and Ingrid Jost, 'Elsheimers unverteilter Nachlass I', in *Simiolus*, I/3, 1967
vG-J II	J. G. van Gelder and Ingrid Jost, 'Elsheimers unverteilter Nachlass II', in *Simiolus*, II/1, 1968
W I	Heinrich Weizsäcker, *Adam Elsheimer, der Maler von Frankfurt*. I (2 vols.). 1936
W II	Heinrich Weizsäcker, *Adam Elsheimer, der Maler von Frankfurt*. II (ed. H. Möhle). 1952
Waddingham 1972	Malcolm Waddingham, 'Elsheimer revised', in *Burlington Magazine*, September 1972

The author and publishers are grateful to all museum authorities and private owne[rs] their possession to be reproduced, and who have also in many cases supplied reproduced by gracious permission of Her Majesty The Queen, and Plates III, 28, of the National Gallery, London.

INDEX OF WORKS

INDEX OF NAMES

Hum
N
6888
E63
A5

FLORIDA STATE UNIVERSITY

3 1254 00877 6516

WITHDRAWN F.S.U.

DATE DUE

NOV 1 0 1993

SEP 2 0 1996

APR 2 6 1997